SUBLIMINAL
COMMUNICATION
EMPEROR'S CLOTHES
OR PANACEA?

SUBLIMINAL COMMUNICATION

EMPEROR'S CLOTHES OR PANACEA?

with How to Create Your Own Subliminal Program

by Eldon Taylor, Ph.D.

**Just
Another
Reality
Box 12419
Las Vegas
Nevada 89112**

*Roy "K" Bey, for support and encouragement
without which this book would not have been possible*

*Lee Liston, for his tireless efforts
within the Utah prison system*

Warren Archer, for cover art

Charles F. McCusker, for abstract of findings

*Richard Erickson, for layout
and book design*

Second Edition

Other books by Eldon Taylor, Ph.D.,
available from this publisher:

Subliminal Learning
Exclusively Fabricated Illusions
The Little Black Book
Subliminal Technology
Simple Things and Simple Thoughts

Withdrawn

CONTENTS

About the Author

Dr. Eldon Taylor is an internationally recognized authority on subliminal communication and for more than twelve years was a practicing criminologist specializing in forensic hypnosis and the detection of deception. His work in the area of subliminal communication was featured in the *Omni Audio Experience* and has been reported in numerous articles in national print publications and on television and radio. He has written dozens of articles and books, recorded hundreds of audiocassettes, contributed chapters to textbooks, and given numerous television and radio interviews. He has earned doctorates in clinical and pastoral psychology and has received many awards. His vita is found in the *International Who's Who of Intellectuals*, published in Cambridge, England, in several other prestigious biographical publications. Dr. Taylor founded Progressive Awareness Research, Inc., and originated the first subliminal research with incarcerated persons.

PREFACE

Thoughts *are* things, and they definitely predispose us to create, if they themselves do not actually create, the realities in our individual lives. The problem, or opportunity, depending upon our perspective, is that many of these thoughts are rooted deeply in the subconscious mind. We may consciously conclude to change this or that, and yet the change turns out to be just another disguise rather than a real change. Sometimes this process in itself gives positive feedback to an undefined subconscious reality, such as failure. That is to say, if our subconscious expects us to fail, the failure is certain. So, we need somehow to get our subconscious to work *for* us.

This work focuses specifically on subliminal communication as a means to do that very thing. But does subliminal communication really work? If it does, what is the evidence? And how does it work? Are there modalities that work better than others? Can subliminal communication create basic changes in personality structure? These and many other questions, implications, and ramifications are treated in the pages that follow. My efforts are not intended to represent the final word. The science of information processing known as subliminal communication is yet too embryonic for definitive answers to every question to have been found. The evidence, however, suggests the need and the opportunity for a variety of interesting research projects. The evidence also shows that subliminal communication works. The questions now should address the variety of modalities, subject matter, length of exposure, "best-time-use" approaches, follow-up studies, and so on.

In our society we are exposed daily to some form of subliminal communication, and our only defense is an informed understanding. To increase this understanding and to use it as a way to develop the yet unexpressed potential that lies dormant within us are the principal objectives of what follows.

CHAPTER ONE

HISTORY

Research into subliminal communication has gone on much longer than one might think. As far back as the turn of the century, some behavioral scientists were using a "whisper" technique in clinical sessions with patients. The idea was, and still is, very simple. If the conscious mind listens to a statement, for the most part it has the prerogative to accept, reject, or modify the statement. For instance, if the conscious mind is told that one feels good, it may argue with the statement. The subconscious mind, however, does not have the same discriminative ability. If the subconscious accepts the suggestion that one feels good, one feels good! Paradoxically, however, the beliefs held in the subconscious are the source of *why* the conscious might reject positive programming. Negative, self-limiting beliefs echo in the subconscious, which instructs the conscious about what is or is not acceptable.

The earliest research into subliminal communication may be that of Suslowa, who in 1863 demonstrated a discrimination threshold relative to subliminal electrical stimulation.

In 1894, W. R. Dunham, M.D., wrote an interesting commentary on the subliminal mind and subliminal communication that nearly one hundred years later still reads to some as though it were science fiction. Following is an excerpt from Dunham's interesting work *The Science of Vital Force:*

1

"The most advanced thinkers have coined the phrase 'subliminal consciousness' as best expressive of an intelligence manifested unlike the ordinary consciousness—an intelligence uprising, as we might say, from a submerged strata of individual personality. And it has been asked, 'Is there some pattern in the very fabric of our nature which begins to show when we scratch the glaze off the stuff?' It may be impossible to define where supraliminal consciousness leaves off, and subliminal intelligence begins; but such, at least, is not our purpose. We only desire . . . to illustrate that there is an obscure feature of human intellectual personality of continued increasing complexity—a kind of intelligence emanating from our obscure selves, of mysterious operation, not easy of comprehension, and for purposes not wholly recognized. . . .

"This sub-state called 'subliminal consciousness' belongs to and is part of the nature of every individual, existing to a more or less degree; and it is capable of being brought to the surface by a system of cultivation. It is not a consciousness which has been acquired through the culture of supraliminal abilities, but a kind of innate consciousness which may acquire intelligence by an entirely different method—a consciousness which may possess wonderful faculties even in persons whose ordinary intelligence may be mediocre and even below par, illustrated frequently in mathematical and musical 'freaks,' so called. It is not unreasonable to suppose that much of the most brilliant genius of historic mention may have been found in persons capable of drawing on this quality of highly endowed natural ability. For this subliminal consciousness, with some individuals, has the ability of silent communication. In other words, the subliminal consciousness of A may learn of the subliminal consciousness of B what might be known by his supraliminal consciousness. Thus A may learn the thought and facts known only to B, which is often accomplished in test proceedings, and is called 'telepathy.' The supraliminal mind may imagine itself, and really be, on any part of the globe, while the subliminal may have even a greater ability: it may describe accurately the things seen; it may enter the residence of persons miles away, and describe all there is in the room as correctly, in many

2

instances, as an individual presence might accomplish. Such feats are called 'clairvoyance'; and clairvoyance consists in a temporary suspension of the supraliminal mind, and the exercise of the subliminal abilities. Hypnotism consists in a temporary suspension of the supraliminal faculties of A, while the supraliminal consciousness of B becomes operative with both the thought and voluntary mechanism of A; and when complete, the voluntary mind of B, with the good subject, may cause hypnotic A to speak the thought of B, while A is not conscious of thus doing.

"But how is this done? The explanation, we fear, would be as difficult as to explain how we think. . . .

"No well-informed person will deny the existence of the alleged subliminal consciousness. Neither is it intellectually prudent to circumscribe the limits and abilities of such division of intellectual function in living human individuality. That agency which has been recognized and given the name of 'psychic force' is a factor of the subliminal consciousness. This comparatively recent discovery of an agency, frequently presented unconsciously through the living human organism, is receiving much attention from the most advanced minds in civilized countries; and to mention the many singular and varied presentations of this agency would require more space than we can give."

In fact, as I suggest in my book *Subliminal Learning,* the information exchange between subjects, and even between subject and object, is holographic. As such, perception per se is in wholes of all units of information. Each unit is unfolding in what we know as the time-space continuum. Thus, even information that is consciously perceived has accompanying it an entire subset of subliminally registered components. The mechanic for this process is what science calls the bioplasma, or corona discharge (commonly known as an aura). Electrophotography, or Kirlian photography, can capture pictures of this bioplasma, which seems to function as a third nervous system, affecting the brain/body organism and reciprocally responding to it. Soviet medicine has successfully used electrophotographs of bioplasma to diagnose and prognosticate both physical and mental disorders. But a discussion of this subject would be

3

a book in itself, and so I return to the history of the use of subliminal communication.

In the 1950s, a New Jersey theater owner reported flashing refreshment subliminals during the showing of the movie *Picnic*. According to claims, flashing the words "Drink Coca-Cola" over Kim Novak's face resulted in a 58 percent increase in Coca-Cola sales over a six-week period.

Vance Packard's work *Hidden Persuaders* appeared in 1957 and, although discredited by many, found itself on the required reading list for many high schools by the late 1960s. Packard quoted from the London *Sunday Times* an account of a New Jersey theater where ice cream ads were flashed onto the screen during a movie showing, resulting in an otherwise unaccountable increase in ice cream sales. The *Times* referred to this technique as "subthreshold effects."

Whether labeled as "subthreshold" or "subliminal," the nature of the communication is such that the conscious mind does not perceive it and, in many instances, could not perceive it. (For a more detailed discussion of semantics and definitions, see Chapter 6.)

Packard's work warned of psychologists turned merchandisers and of the resulting psychoseduction of the American consumer. From belief systems to product identification, Packard presented a case for persuasion through the art and science of motivational analysis, feedback, and psychological manipulation. *Hidden Persuaders* was the first open attempt to inform the general public of a potentially Orwellian means to enslave the mind and to do so surreptitiously.

Since the New Jersey theater accounts, headline stories have appeared in nearly all major publications reporting the use of subliminal techniques. The subject matter of these stories ranges from sports motivation to the reduction of pilferage.

By 1980, the McDonagh Medical Clinic in Gladstone, Missouri, had installed a subliminal processor to mix spoken words at an imperceptible level with music to relax patients. The clinic reported a decrease in patient anxiety levels, attested to by the absence of fainting. When the subliminal message was removed, patients began fainting again.

4

How far back the use of subliminal communication reaches and in what guises it is affecting each of us today makes interesting conjecture. It is asserted that Alfred Hitchcock inserted subliminal words such as *blood, knife,* and *murder* in the first release of the movie *Psycho* for the purpose of heightening fear in the audience.

So far as I can ascertain, the earliest use of audio subthreshold communication (aside from the whisper therapy mentioned earlier) was employed by Lozanov in Bulgaria to enhance learning abilities in language and mathematics. Lozanov's technique put much more emphasis on other aspects of what has become known as suggestopedia, however, than it did on the use of subliminals.

Then along came the Becker "black box." Dr. Becker, formerly a professor at Tulane University, patented a "little black box" that mixed spoken words with Muzak at levels subaudible to the conscious mind. (For more on the Becker process, see Chapter 6 regarding the process of creating audiosubliminals.) Becker's box was initially tested in department stores where messages such as "I am honest" and "I will not steal" were credited with dramatic reductions in inventory shrinkages.

Wilson Brian Key, who has been charged by critics with having a "dirty mind" and thereby reading filth into what Key charges are sexually exploitive ads, illustrates in his work *Clam Plate Orgy* subliminal and supraliminal content in advertising and art going back as far as the Sistine Chapel (*supraliminal* referring to consciously unnoticed, *subliminal* to consciously not perceivable).

One individual I have spoken with was personally involved in back-masking messages related to drugs and satanic worship for various rock groups in the early seventies. (Back-masking is a technique commonly used to combine subliminal audio tracks with music; see Chapter 6 for details.) According to this person, he stopped doing this when the messages became observable in fans' behavior. The groups, including such well-known ones as KISS, reportedly came up with the idea from some old Eastern literature as yet unidentified.

5

At the time of this writing, a legal case is unfolding in the Nevada courts in which is it alleged that the heavy-metal group Judas Priest created a recording that contained subliminal messages directing listeners to commit suicide. The plaintiffs contend that these messages led to the death of one young fan and the maiming of another. The court has many precedent-setting issues before it, involving First Amendment rights and technical creative nuances. One issue arising out of the latter has to do with the electronic recoverability of subliminal content. In a recent telephone consultation with an expert involved in the case, I expressed my opinion that if the subliminal content is not electronically retrievable, then it is insufficient to be registered by the brain at all. To be subliminally registered, a stimulus must be sufficient to trigger the "firing" of a neuron: a whisper two blocks away is not a subliminal stimulus because it is insufficient to trigger that process in the brain. Still, certain masking techniques can make the recovery of subliminal messages extremely challenging.

There is no doubt that messages such as "Kill yourself . . . do it now," whether subliminally or supraliminally presented, can combine with certain personality instabilities or disorders to evoke the response of suicide. It is my further opinion that messaging of this kind is not only irresponsible but criminal, and it should be subject to criminal penalties as well as to civil remedies.

However far back subliminals were used and however actively they are currently being used, it is nearly impossible to imagine an individual in today's population who has not been exposed to subliminal persuasion techniques of one kind or another. Asking how *much* subliminal messaging we are all products of is much more relevant than asking whether we have been subliminally manipulated. For that matter, I would consider it a fair question, after you examine the cover to this book closely, for you to ask yourself whether or not the word *sex* embedded in the cover illustration had anything to do with your acquiring this book. (See Appendix A.)

6

CHAPTER TWO

MECHANICS

Many times I have been asked to explain how a sexual sub-liminal or a horror subliminal can sell a product for an adver-tiser. I always begin my answer by referring the questioner (as I now refer you) to Professor Key's work *Subliminal Seduc-tion.* Key spends a great deal of effort explaining the various psychological mechanisms that make erotic, violent, and gen-erally consciously disgusting material profitable to ad makers. Perhaps most important among them is the repression mecha-nism. Simply stated, and unbelievable as you may find this, the repression mechanism functions so that we see only what we want to see. Now, this is an oversimplification but worth repeat-ing: we see what we want to see and fail to see often explicit content that our own beliefs and expectations prohibit us from seeing.

For example, once while attempting to explain this process to a group of inmates at the Utah State Prison, I passed among the inmate audience a *Playboy* subscription advertisement that appeared in *Subliminal Seduction.* The advertisement portrays a beautiful naked blonde female with a Christmas wreath. Writ-ten in the center of the wreath is the statement, "Give him ideas for Christmas." The wreath appears to be made of wal-nuts. On close inspection, however, the wreath clearly pictures penis heads and vaginas. The inmates, like the readers of *Play-boy,* where the advertisement originally appeared, were consciously unaware of the sexual communication that occurred at a subconscious level, even when they were instructed to search specifically for such content.

It could be argued that at least two reasons are behind using this type of ad. The most obvious is that the subliminal content increases the length of time the viewer looks at an advertisement. The second reason is a little more complicated and essentially consists of two parts. The first relates to recall or product identification at point of purchase and the other to some nonconscious excitability that has been linked subliminally to the product.

Thus, perceptual defense mechanisms ranging from repression to sublimination serve as lenses to protect us against perceptual damage. It might be valuable to review the basic perceptual defense mechanisms.

Denial. As implied by its name, this mechanism is simply one of denying. Often the denial occurs through projection, that is, projecting blame or fault onto another.

Fantasy formation. This mechanism creates a perceived reality out of fantasy. If motives cannot be satisfied in the objective external world, they may become a perceived reality in a dream world. Some psychologists suggest that the appeal for much of our entertainment is oriented to satisfying our fantasies for adventure, affection, and security, perhaps not so vividly experienced otherwise.

Introjection. This mechanism allows one to place blame on oneself. This self-directed blame or punishment defends against disappointment or disillusionment in another. For example, a child feels unworthy of the parent's attention because the parent pays no attention to the child.

Isolation. This mechanism involves the avoidance of connecting associations to related ideas that produce anxiety. One set of data is isolated from an associated set: birth is isolated from death, war from mourning, nuclear arsenals from murderous horror, and so forth.

Projection. Simply stated, this mechanism allows one to project blame or responsibility onto another.

Regression. This mechanism is common during serious illness. Essentially, one regresses to an earlier age, usually as a dependent, where one felt safe and comfortable. The individual usually returns to an earlier stage of development where someone else assumed responsibility and where fewer, simpler, and more primitive goals existed.

Repression. Generally this mechanism censors or prohibits memories, associations, and adjustments from conscious awareness. Like an invisible filter, this mechanism prevents the conscious mind from "seeing" painful memories and "stymied" motives. Personal experiences ranging from embarrassment to cruelty are often subject to the lens of repression.

Sublimation. This mechanism redirects basic drive mechanisms. Sublimation is simply the substitution of acceptable behavior to satisfy basic motives that might be met equally well in a primitive sense by some form of unacceptable social behavior. Aggression motives, for instance, are often met by sports activities. The process of sublimation is to find avenues in which basic motives may be satisfied in a manner acceptable to the individual and to society. The sublimation of what is termed the Oedipus complex (sexual desire for a parent) led to the production of much of the scientific literature about subliminal communication, and it is behind the success of the symbiotic message. (See Chapter 7.)

In addition to these eight mechanisms, there are several miscellaneous escapes and defenses that some theorists consider as contributing to the basic perceptual defenses outlined above, all for the purpose of showing each of us only what we want to see about ourselves and about the world around us. It should be noted also that several mechanisms can function at one time; in that case, the boundaries overlap, making it difficult to differentiate between the mechanisms.

Repeated experiments have adequately demonstrated that the conscious mind is not a necessary part of information processing. In fact, the unconscious can and quite frequently does operate without, or at least unknown to, the conscious. Freud once stated that "the most complicated achievements of thought are possible without the assistance of consciousness."

9

He further asserted that the will and volition of the conscious govern only conscious mental processes and that every compulsion is rooted in the subconscious.

Where preconscious predisposition is concerned, Benjamin Libet of the University of California believes that conscious intention only facilitates or inhibits action initiated by the preconscious process. In fact, according to the *Brain-Mind Bulletin*'s report on Libet's work, correlates between EEG patterns and conscious experience reveal that 350 milliseconds before the subjective experience of, say, wanting to move, distinct activity in brain wave patterns occurs. Libet views this model as understanding choice. One chooses to act or not to act. One does not necessarily choose what to act upon.

It is noteworthy that research has confirmed an increase in brain wave pattern activity in test subjects who listened to music containing a subliminal message over the pattern activity in test subjects who listened to the same music without the hidden messages. Without conscious awareness, the brain appeared to be processing and otherwise responding to unconscious stimuli. (See *Subliminal Learning* for more information.)

It is also noteworthy that Robert Chapman at the University of Rochester demonstrated that words grouped according to connotation—for example, *beautiful* (a "good" word) and *crime* (a "bad" word)—elicited distinctive gross EEG patterns. Moreover, the patterns were substantially similar between different subjects from diverse cultures.

Dr. Poetzle is credited with contributing one of the first scientifically meaningful findings regarding subliminal communication. Poetzle, working with dream content, discovered that material perceived consciously does not appear in dreams. Information and stimuli appearing in dreams are apparently drawn from stimuli unconsciously perceived prior to the dream. Poetzle therefore concluded that dream content is primarily constructed from subliminally perceived material. Poetzle further demonstrated that a conscious association could stimulate a subliminal perception even years after the perception occurred.

Phraseology such as *subliminal perception* seems awkward because the terms are mutually exclusive. In this usage, however, the meaning of *perception* is stretched to include any level of

10

perception—conscious or unconscious. Research clearly shows that somehow information is processed from stimuli received but not consciously perceived. Thus, stretching the literal meaning of the word *perception* is convenient, and *perception* is used here in that enlarged sense. Technically, though, what occurs is the *registration* of the stimulus in the unconscious rather than the *perception* of the stimulus.

Data assembled by psychologists and neurologists strongly support the notion that all sensory input comes through at least two levels of perception—conscious and unconscious. And more than one notable thinker is of the opinion that no significant belief originates from data consciously perceived.

From Poetzle's work in the early 1900s to now, subliminal perception has been tested and retested. The results are conclusive. Human activity can be affected by subliminally perceived material in at least eight areas: conscious perception, dreams, drives, emotions, memory, perceptual defenses, value norm anchor points, and verbal behavior.

The purpose here is not to treat psychological functions or the nature of consciousness itself. There are volumes by prominent authorities on those subjects. The purpose here is to give a straightforward, simplified account to demonstrate how subliminal communication has been and is being accomplished. Despite the "Missourian" mentality of "show me," the emperor is wearing clothes. Subliminal communication is real!

I have often been asked, "Do you really believe this stuff?" The answer is, Absolutely! The actual mental mechanics are subject to theory and controversy, but then, so is the nature of consciousness. In fact, I am reminded of Theodor Reik's observation about the controversy over the nature of attention, one of the states of consciousness: Is it an activity or a state or a pseudo-conception of a nonexistence?

Much work is going on right now in the various areas and interfaces of behavioral science to produce a better understanding of how unseen, unheard, unconscious influences are perceived and integrated into consciousness. The question is no longer whether subliminal communication exists but rather how it works. As with gravity, electricity, or consciousness itself, our explanations are often at best observation points of seen influences interpreted as theories about unseen reality.

11

CHAPTER THREE

THE LAW AND SUBLIMINALS

Most people are surprised to learn that there are no laws regulating subliminal communication. There is no protection from subliminal manipulation or legal appeal other than the possibility of civil remedy. Perhaps the Judas Priest case discussed in Chapter 1 will break ground in providing the basis for criminal penalties for detrimental use of subliminal communication.

If it were not unconscionable that nothing has ever been written into law to prohibit subliminal exploitation, it would be amusing. The public reaction of the late fifties and early sixties ended where it began. What was considered by *Newsday* as "the most alarming invention since the atomic bomb" has been shuffled away to "dirty mind" arguments and ghosts that go bump in the night. Those who knew laws actually had not been placed on the books were made to believe that what you could not hear could not hurt you. What you could not see, you did not see, because it was not there.

In numerous interviews and interactions with the public, I have been continually astounded by the number of people who have simply relegated subliminals either to category one—they don't work; they're like the emperor's clothes in the fairytale;

call it placebo or call it pretend—or to category two—they're against the law.

Although several states and even the United States Senate have introduced legislation to prohibit subliminals in public communication media, no legislation has ever been enacted.

In 1986, Representative Frances Merrill of the Utah House of Representatives initiated legislation to prohibit subliminal communication without informed consent.

The intent of Representative Merrill's proposed legislation, remember, was to prohibit subliminal exposure without informed consent. In other words, just as restaurants years ago posted notices regarding microwave use, a retailer using antitheft subliminals, for example, would be required to inform those who might hear the tapes. Obviously, heavy-metal music groups using subliminals also would be required to display appropriate notices, as would any and all other users of subliminal communication.

There were three bills in all, H.B. 106, 107, and 108. (The exact wording of the house bills as originally proposed is given in Appendix B.) As had been the case with past attempts at legislation to regulate subliminals, the proposed legislation met with much opposition, and discussion in Utah House committee meetings was often heated.

The same week the House committee reviewed Representative Merrill's legislation, the *Wall Street Journal* reported that Uncle Sam was using subliminal "Mom" messages to calm workers' nerves. Several studies were made available to the committee demonstrating clearly the efficacy of subliminal technology.

On the first day of the committee's deliberation, Barbara Levy, speaking on behalf of the American Association of Advertising Agencies, equated subliminals with ink blot tests, flatly claiming that people can find anything in them. Levy stated, "Subliminal advertising is a myth perpetuated by a few confused consumers."

Terry Jessop, who is the founder and head of the National Institute of Subliminal Research and who suggested the bills to Representative Merrill, said, "Ninety-nine percent of all ad agen-

13

cies are totally ethical. . . . The basic issue is the right of privacy. A person has a right to his own mind.''

Representative Merrill stated that she was concerned about brainwashing.

Chief among the opponents to the legislation was Virgil Hayes, identified as president of the Rocky Mountain Hypnotists Examining Council. Hayes argued that the bills were ambiguous.

At my invitation, the argument was taken to the airwaves for public interaction. The Salt Lake City talk radio station, KTKK, and its evening host, Jim Kirkwood, agreed to a two-hour open discussion. Joining Mr. Kirkwood and me were Representative Merrill, Mr. Jessop, and Mr. Hayes. (Highlights of the program, quoted from a transcript of the broadcast, are given in Appendix C.) In my opinion, it is worthy of mention that after the radio discussion I learned that Mr. Hayes, an outspoken opponent of the legislation, has a company that installs subliminal mixers in businesses for the purpose of broadcasting subliminal messages in their music system.

After the radio broadcast, two amendments were offered by Representative Merrill to clarify ambiguities in the bills as originally written. (See Appendix D.)

The committee heard final statements before voting. I had prepared a written summary of our position, and a spokesperson delivered it orally:

"We specialize in self-help products. Every day I hear testimonies regarding the efficacy of subliminal products—we know subliminals work.

"It has been argued that they do not and even suggested that it takes a dirty mind to find the 'alleged subliminal.' It has been stated that there is no scientific evidence regarding subliminals. These statements are simply untrue. There is an abundance of literature regarding subliminals. One such scientific study, conducted by Dr. Hal Becker, former professor of Tulane University, exposed subjects to numbers subliminally. Where this was done the subjects scored 80 percent correctly when asked to identify the numbers. (May I add that three-digit numbers were used). Chance alone was less than 20 percent based upon

14

the multiple-choice nature of the selection alternatives. And in groups where subliminals were not used, only about 10 percent identified the three-digit numbers correctly.

"Now, as far as the dirty-mind argument is concerned: That is an argument of association. In other words, if you and I find a subliminal that is a taboo, a sex embed, we must have a dirty mind. So what—we pretend not to see what we see? That sounds like conscious repression to me. And as far as subliminals found in some heavy-metal recordings like 'Smoke Marijuana' and 'Commit Suicide,' even *60 Minutes* has presented exposes documenting this.

"In the mid-1950s a New Jersey theater owner claimed to increase Coke sales 58 percent via subliminals. The controversy resulted in over forty states introducing some kind of legislation—none of which ever became law. There have always been essentially three arguments that have defeated it. They are:

"1. The 'dirty-mind argument.'

"2. The 'they don't work argument,' and that is interesting with the scientific and clinical data now available, for if they don't work, why oppose them?

"3. Finally, the vague and ambiguous argument, that I have saved for last. Yes, the language by definition of subliminal communication is too broad in its extreme sense of interpretation. Twenty-eight years later, there still exists *no* definition to communicate what we all know is trying to be communicated in the intent of Representative Merrill's bills. But someone has to define it.

"There are some bills that need to be exposed to rigorous debate and amendment from the entire floor of the House. This is one such bill. There is no technology with more Orwellian possibilities than subliminal communication. We are all entitled to be informed of what subliminal manipulation is present and when present.

"There are no virtues to deliberate exploitation by any means, including the intentional misuse of subliminal communication. For that reason we support H.B. 106 and 107.

"Thank you."

The committee narrowly approved the proposed legislation to go to the House floor, but the House voted it down. To this date there still exists no legal protection against subliminal invasion of privacy.

CHAPTER FOUR

TESTIMONIES

Thousands of personal testimonies exist concerning subliminal self-improvement programs. Every manufacturer of subliminals sells its product to some extent because of personal testimonies.

But science is not fond of testimonies per se. A number of variables, including the well-known placebo effect, dilute the "scientific" value of any testimony. Science often scoffs at claims based upon personal experience. To most scientists, where the scientific method and adequate controls are absent, so is the credibility of the experience. The interesting double bind here is that science now knows there is not such a thing as the observed without the observer and, moreover, the observer is a participant in the event being observed. Nevertheless, science argues for a difference between trained and untrained observers.

A dear friend of mine, William Guillory, a professor of physical chemistry, has on many occasions flatly asserted that there are no "truths" in science. Science itself is a tautology. For example, consider life itself as a phenomenon. Consider further that at the moment of death, no *physical* quality has changed—not weight, not chemistry—yet life is gone. Life itself appears to be metaphysical. Our most basic assumptions are based upon principles that in and of themselves cannot be proven or explained except by observation.

Chapters 5 and 6 treat scientific proof, but it is my opinion that users' testimony is not only credible but also of value in ascertaining the most meaningful areas to direct any scientific research. For example, users occasionally report resistances to subliminal programs. Scientists should examine these reports, seeking more insight into the dynamics of the resistance.

To me, science is and should be, at least in part, like the FDA. The purpose of that agency is to protect us from unsafe pharmaceuticals. This is a consumer-based function. The user dictates what is or is not meaningful, and science attests to its independent or universal validity. The fact that a placebo alters body chemistry just as pharmaceuticals might alter the body chemistry of an individual or of a certain percentage of a group of individuals makes a statement that is meaningful to all, not just to the individual experiencing relief from some physiological dysfunction. When the placebo provides the same relief for the vast majority as pharmaceuticals provide, it can no longer be considered a placebo. At that point science should further examine its properties to ascertain the whys and hows inherent in its universal application and the resulting relief brought about by its properties.

In my view, genius in science is always found where the scientist investigates anomalies. Breakthroughs come from looking more at exceptions than at rules. The following testimonies represent such anomalies and exceptions and, consequently, should spark thorough scientific investigation.

Marilee had more than two hundred warts on her hands. Over the years she had many of them burned off. After using a subliminal wart-removal audiotape for thirty days, the warts were all gone. Six months later the warts had not returned.

Diana Steed used a subliminal bust-enlargement audiotape and reported "amazing" results.

Mike Anglesey chewed his nails down to the quick for fifteen years. A number of stop/prevention programs had been tried by Anglesey without results. After three weeks of listening to a stop-nail-biting subliminal audiotape, he stopped and had not restarted six months later.

18

Judee Goddard purchased a subliminal weight-loss audiotape to play surreptitiously to her husband. After thirty days, Mr. Goddard had lost twenty-six pounds. Mrs. Goddard did not inform her husband about the subliminal program.

An unnamed woman reported playing her weight-loss subliminal program while preparing dinner. After several exposures, she observed that her twenty-month-old baby had stopped eating his dinner. She discontinued use of the audiotape while her child was present.

Where children are concerned, the age at which a word becomes meaningful to them as a word is an area of relevant inquiry. Peter Eimas of Brown University has amassed considerable evidence suggesting that a child one month of age can distinguish some differences in words. In light of this finding, the question of subliminal exposure to very young children takes on a different dimension.

To placate his wife, Dempsey Whitaker, a heavy smoker for thirty-eight years, agreed to listen to a subliminal stop-smoking audiotape. Whitaker stated that he was not ready to stop smoking but that he would listen to the tape. After seven days, Whitaker no longer wanted a cigarette, and one year later Whitaker remains a nonsmoker.

Mrs. X was involved in an auto accident. Physical therapy was required for rehabilitation. The therapy, basically stretching exercises, was impossible for Mrs. X to do until she used a joy-of-exercise subliminal her daughter had purchased. After that the therapy was accomplished without psychological or physiological side effects.

Vern Water's mother, a social worker, purchased a stop-loss-of-hair tape for Vern. Vern had already lost most of his hair in what appeared to be classical male-pattern baldness. After listening for less than one month, Vern began to grow new hair. After approximately two months, Vern once again had a full head of hair; however, one year later the baldness pattern had returned.

Arnold Stringham suffered from migraine headaches for years. After he used a subliminal migraine-relief program for less than thirty days, the headaches ceased. So convinced is Stringham of the efficacy of subliminal programs that he now uses them in a real estate school he instructs, and he claims a statistically significant increase in the number of students passing the state examination as a result. Part of Stringham's first day of instruction with a new class is spent explaining subliminals, relating his experiences, recommending the audiotapes, and then commencing to play various learning programs.

Robert Youngblood, M.D., asserts that the use of subliminal relaxation and wellness messages are assisting patients before and after surgery. Additionally, one of his staff used a stop-bed-wetting tape on a chronic bed wetter (a boy, age fourteen) and ended the bed wetting.

On numerous occasions I have heard of medical "miracles," including a number of cancer remissions.

Beverly E., an educator specializing in teaching the learning disabled, reported a 300 percent average improvement in tested grade-level competency as a result of using subliminal programs and guided imagery with her students.

A free-standing psychiatric center reported a noticeable difference in levels of aggression and hostility in adolescent patients exposed to subliminal messaging.

L. L. introduced pain control subliminal programs into a hospice. At least one patient previously in uncontrollable pain reduced the dosage of chemical pain relievers and successfully upgraded his freedom from pain by using a subliminal program.

C. M. played a subliminal self-healing audiotape to a comatose patient and credited the patient's seemingly miraculous recovery to the messages on the tape.

J. L.'s son was younger and smaller than the children he went to school with, but he wanted to be on the wrestling team. J. L. purchased a special wrestling tape for her son. He not only made the team but went to the championship matches. He and his family credited the subliminal program as the factor that made the difference.

Dr. J. S. experimented with subliminal audiotapes by using them on doctoral candidates while he instructed a "difficult chemistry class." He reported that there was no doubt about the marked improvement of the students, as attested by their examination scores.

David's teenaged son had a drug problem. David purchased a drug-free subliminal program, and his son agreed to play it. David's son is drug free today.

L. P.'s son had a behavioral disorder and was failing in school. Subliminal programs designed for successful children were employed. Today this young man is an excellent student who has left his behavioral problems behind. His mother stated that she would play the programs at bedtime, and soon the boy was requesting them.

Many offices have reported increasing production and decreasing stress and costs related to health care as a result of playing subliminal messages in the office music system.

A surgeon reported a significant decrease in the amount of anesthetic required for patients who listened to a special pre-operative subliminal program.

R. L.'s mother-in-law used a subliminal program entitled *Clean, Neat, and Tidy.* She reported discontinuing its use after three days because she was fatigued from continual housecleaning. (This woman was in her late seventies.)

J. P. reported "hiding" her intimacy program when her husband, who had no idea it had been being used, became so amorous that he "would not leave me alone."

A gentleman played an anti-procrastination subliminal program at bedtime on the first evening after he purchased it. According to him, he soon got out of bed and cleaned the garage until 3 A.M., when he finally could go back to sleep. He felt strongly that the program should have had a statement warning against its use at bedtime.

C. S. reported experiencing spontaneous astral projections, or "out of body" experience, as a result of using a subliminal audiotape intended to awaken psychic abilities.

Some companies offer a few subliminal programs designed to enhance extrasensory perception or to teach specific parapsychological skills. Sometimes users ask whether using these subliminal properties makes them more open to paranormal impressions. The answer seems a bit complicated, for much

21

evidence exists to show a correlation between "psychic" people and persons who can perceive a subliminal message. Theoretically the mind can be trained to be more aware of the subtle energies surrounding us. Some evidence in my own research suggests that the more one listens to properly recorded subliminal programs, the more one "hears" the subliminal content. This is not to say, however, that one who listens to subliminal programs designed to enhance their psychic abilities becomes more vulnerable to paranormal impressions. Indeed, the more one is *aware* of input, regardless of its origin or energy level, the more one's discriminative abilities can be employed. If, as has been suggested, children possess more psychic abilities than adults do, then it is probably so because children are more in tune with all of their sense mechanisms.

What may occur with the use of subliminal programs is a return to natural sensing as opposed to learned and analyzed sensing. Dr. Russel Targ, a noted investigator into psychic phenomena, told me that analysis inhibited the accuracy of impressions in studies involving remote viewing and precognition. Targ suggested that the best psi scores are obtained from those who state that they do not possess psychic ability and the worst scores are generally obtained from those who state that they do possess psychic abilities. (He further suggested that this correlation could be caused by fears, such as fear of failure.) One example of this correlation occurred later in the week of this conversation at the psychotronic convention Targ and I were attending. After a spoon-bending party, a well-known author and investigator into psychic phenomena, who many consider to have psychic ability, was reported to have been embarrassed by his inability to use his psychic powers to bend a spoon; whereas a reporter from the *National Enquirer,* a very intelligent, probing, and "show me" writer, easily bent her spoon.

I have heard testimonies from hundreds of users of subliminal purporting to have improved memory, test-taking skills, learning abilities, and concentration; to have removed warts, ended migraines, enlarged breasts, promoted healing; to have ended insomnia, provided relief from allergies, and so on. Many times I have been asked, "How does a subliminal program do this?"

The subliminal programs do not *do* anything other than provide the mind with stimuli that the mind acts upon. The mind is the doer! In fact, the subliminal messages may be argued to do no more than facilitate a condition of "true belief." With "true belief" well established in the mind, the body responds. (The concept of the mind as healer or slayer is not a new one.) As with any placebo, "true belief," or the expectation of success, must be present for a placebo effect to occur. Whether the subliminal program creates a placebo effect or is itself a placebo is a futile and circular inquiry. The fact is that statistically placebos are successful in approximately 20 percent of cases; users of subliminal programs report efficacy in more than 80 percent of cases.

There can be contraindications to the use of subliminal programs, however. For example, the use of a subliminal relaxation program while one is operating a car or heavy machinery is contraindicated because of the obvious possibility of drowsiness. A medical or emotional condition might require the user of certain subliminal programs to have close professional supervision. For a discussion of these contraindications, examples, and case studies, please see *Subliminal Learning.*

23

CHAPTER FIVE

THE CLINICAL DATA

Eight areas of human activity were identified in Chapter 2 as having been demonstrably affected by subliminal communication. Once again, these areas are conscious perception, dreams, drives, emotions, memory, perceptual defenses, value norm anchor points, and verbal behavior. In *Subliminal Seduction,* Professor Key illustrates each of these areas as they are affected and even exploited through subliminal communication techniques. I highly recommend Key's work; however, because the purpose of this volume is not so much to look at media exploitation as to distinguish credible information from the hype, only a cursory review of Key's material is appropriate here.

Conscious perception presupposes that the way one sees the world is through a system of "sets." Most behavioral scientists credit the enculturation process with giving us this predisposition, and the sets are often regarded by political scientists as ethnocentric. Means for evaluating and coping with good and bad, right and wrong, within a society are constructed through the use of sets. For example, facial expressions and body language in general are often paired with language to give rise to different meanings. According to Key, interpretation of facial expressions has been demonstrated to be influenceable by subliminal stimuli. In other words, an essentially expressionless face can be seen as having an angry expression if the viewer is exposed simultaneously to the word *anger* at a subliminal level.

Dreams constitute one of our clearest empirical accesses to unconscious processes. As was discussed in Chapter 2 in a review of some of Poetzle's work, dreams often process subliminally perceived stimuli. Key cites several instances of individuals' dreaming "out" subliminally perceived stimuli embedded in commercial advertising. Key also suggests that subliminal perception is close kin to posthypnotic suggestion. Because posthypnotic suggestions can be and often are erased from conscious awareness by another suggestion for partial amnesia, Key suggests that the functional aspect of both are more alike than not.

As a hypnotist myself, I am aware of applications in which subliminal communication is employed simultaneously with trance therapy to effect beneficial changes in a client. Very often a dichotic approach is preferred for light hypnotic subjects. For example, a hypnotherapist may use a verbal dialogue suggesting to clients that it's okay to feel good about themselves while the hypnotherapist simultaneously plays an audio track that under gentle ocean sounds is flatly stating subliminally, "I do feel good about myself." (See Chapters 7 and 8; see also *Subliminal Learning* for a review and discussion of the dichotic, or "whole brain," technique, which uses permissive and authoritarian statements simultaneously.)

Dreams very often are passages to otherwise hidden unresolved conflict. It is not at all uncommon for a patient to report a dream that brings this conflict to the surface after a session using a dichotic or amnesive approach as an uncovering technique; but that can also be said for any other normally acceptable therapeutic intervention or uncovering modality.

Emotions are among the most responsive of all human behavioral characteristics to be affected by subliminal communication. The ability of subliminal messages to excite, arouse, or anger us or to desensitize us to external stimuli is well established in the literature and will be discussed in more detail later in this chapter when we look at specific clinical data.

Memory also has been increased by the aid of subliminal perception. The Lozanov material, for instance, was mentioned in Chapter 1. The "superlearning" formats, as they have become known, largely because of the work of Lynn Schroeder and Sheila Ostrander, whether called suggestology, suggestopedia, sophrology, or accelerated learning, usually incorporate both some form of altered (alpha) consciousness and subliminal techniques.

It should also be noted that memory is a complex process. Ordinarily, discussion is about conscious memory, but unconscious memory also exists. Because our defense mechanisms function the way they do, many memories become undesirable and are stored away in the unconscious. It can be further said that many one-time useful memories have also slipped out of conscious memory into the subconscious/unconscious. There is also unconscious processing going on that the conscious never is aware of. These too may contribute to unconscious memories.

The exploiters of subliminal techniques usually will appeal more to the unconscious level of memory in their manipulative merchandising. If the amount of money spent on such merchandising indicates the success of this type of marketing strategy, this form of subliminal communication is *very* effective.

There is also associative memory, that is, memory of something consciously perceived because of stimuli simultaneously unconsciously perceived and yet connectively associated. One good, although in my opinion irresponsible, example of the subliminal use of associative memory is an experiment carried out by educational psychologist Dr. Bruce R. Ledford, who theorized that if advertisers could increase product identification, then, in a similar manner, learning could be enhanced. Ledford proceeded to expose students at East Texas State University to erotic and violent pictures projected subliminally on a screen behind him as he lectured. The slides were shown at one candlepower below the light in the classroom and were therefore consciously imperceptible. Ledford's lectures, which had nothing to do with the slides being projected, were apparently more interesting to the students than in the past, as reflected by test scores. Test results indicated in the experimental group a significant increase in memory relevant to the material presented by Ledford over the memory of a control group of students who viewed only a blank screen behind Ledford's lectern.

Perceptual defenses protect us from shocking or deeply traumatic material. Our perceptual defenses can actually assist a subliminal manipulation by shutting out data we might otherwise perceive. Tantamount to this is Key's example of the menu in his *Clam Plate Orgy*. An orgy scene is not what one expects to find in an illustration of a plate of clams on a menu in a prominent and respected restaurant. Simply speaking, we refuse to see what is there to be seen.

Value norm anchor point is a position selected by an individual as a referent point between opposites. It is from such points that he evaluates himself and the world around him. The value norm anchor point is a personally/culturally accepted position between good and bad, right and wrong, success and failure, approval and rejection, and so forth. Numerous studies report that subliminally perceived data can move these anchor points around.

As a criminologist, for years I regularly interacted with people whom society refers to as criminals, thieves, and so on. One thing I observed quickly: no one believes himself to be bad. Now that may be an overgeneralization, but essentially everyone rationalizes away deviant behavior through one or more of the defense mechanisms. Truth requires facing responsibility at some level of reality. Accepting self-responsibility is more often than not counter to the motives of our defense mechanisms.

Have you ever asked yourself why a person confesses a crime? I have conducted hundreds of lie detection tests and taken hundreds of confessions. Not once did the examinee come into my office with a confession on his or her lips. Denial, denial, denial is the point at which all interrogations begin.

Good interrogators learn to read every aspect of communication, from word count to body language. They also understand and use the defense mechanisms. For example, an interrogator may suggest to a person suspected of stealing from an employer that the employer was harsh and unfair, thereby affording the suspect empathy and an opportunity to rationalize his or her behavior by placing blame on the employer. In other words, the employer deserved it! Had he been fair, he would have paid the suspect more and not stolen time and in other ways taken advantage of the employee to the extent that it became okay to "get even" with the employer.

In a discussion one day, an associate informed me of a study of subliminals used in conjunction with lie detection. His report piqued my interest. Could a subliminal be used to soften a value norm anchor point and produce a new reference on the truthful end of the truth/lie continuum? Despite my efforts to locate the study, I was not successful. Subsequently I decided to experiment on my own by using a subliminal audiotape containing harp and flute music with subaudible words from the Twenty-third Psalm.

After playing this tape during a number of interrogations, I observed striking differences in length of interrogation time, confession ratios to deception-indicated charts, and pretest admissions. The Twenty-third Psalm had made my work much easier. Why would the Twenty-third Psalm move a value norm anchor point in a member of our culture? The answer is obvious, and the reason I suggest it is that the confessions became sincere admissions of wrongdoing as opposed to rationalized statements regarding a specific conduct. The real question is, then, Would it do the same in a non-Christian culture?

One other noticeable difference was evident with the use of the Twenty-third Psalm. Situational stress and general anxiety levels in all subjects were reduced.

Now, this is experiential data—not scientific proof. Nevertheless, two other examiners have reported findings similar to mine as a result of using this same subliminal audiocassette.

Verbal behavior is a complex construct. At least three aspects should be considered in relation to the use of subliminals:

1. Multiple meaning permutations
2. Explicit/implicit set
3. Contextual reference

Multiple meaning permutations refer to words that contain other words with drastically different meanings, such as the *con* in *confidence,* and to implications or associations, such as the noun *pea* and the verb *pee*. Key, in *Subliminal Seduction,* states that certain taboo four-letter words are also implied in seemingly innocuous verbiage. Key selected such words as *whose (whore)* and *cult (cunt)* to demonstrate strong emotional responses at a subliminal level. Key claims that words of this nature are deliberately used in ad copy to build emotional content. Key also refers to a broad scope of experiments that demonstrate that these emotion-laden words evoke physiological responses that can be measured on an electroencephalograph.

It should be noted, however, that according to the work of Warren Brown and James Murch of UCLA, words that sound similar, such as *rose* and *rows,* consistently produce different brain wave patterns.

Explicit/implicit set refers to definitions of words or terms. For example, if you say, ''I am honest,'' you mean that you do honest behaviors and also that you do not do dishonest behaviors. In other words, you define *honest* both by what you include in the definition and by what you exclude.

Furthermore, language involves both explicit denotations and implicit connotations. Take, for instance, the word *occult.* For most people this word has associations of ''satanic''; the dictionary, however, says *occult* means ''not disclosed; kept secret; communicated only to the initiated. *Early science:* not apparent on mere inspection but discoverable by experimentation.''

Contextual reference employs both the denotative and the connotative values attached to a word or term to give it particular meaning in a given context. For example, a politician may use the word *liberty* in a speech to evoke in the voters the strong, positive values most people associate with that word. A close comparison of the politician's actions with his rhetoric will show his constituents whether or not *liberty* meant the same thing to him as it did to them.

In summary, then, subliminal communication has had demonstrable effects on the eight areas of human activity just discussed. But clinical data suggests there are other areas of human activity that subliminal communication can and does affect. The Soviets, for example, are reported to have been working on subliminal condition/response for years. Subliminals have been found to influence skin temperature, galvanic skin response, heartbeat—in fact, most of our physiological processes, if not all of them.

In 1983, one manufacturer reported to me that his company had created a subliminal for use by law enforcement personnel in terrorist abductions, that it had been tested, and that it worked. The subliminal was designed to bring about dysfunctions of the bladder, liver, and kidneys. The manufacturer explained that statistics indicated that in terrorist abductions, hours were spent on the telephone in negotiation with the terrorists. The idea was to create a subliminal and cover the audio track with pink sound— in this instance, the sound of air conditioning. He claimed that the tape was tested at an unidentified police academy under medical supervision but was employed covertly. After three days, the subliminal was removed. The result of the test was that nearly the entire class of cadets became dehydrated.

Subliminals have been demonstrated to affect the perception threshold. Ostrander and Schroeder relate in their *Subliminal Report* that when words with unsavory connotations were subliminally presented to one eye, the perception threshold of the other eye was increased.

Subliminals can influence addictive behavior. A doctoral student of Thomas Budzynski's studied subliminal input and its effect on alcoholics. Groups treated with subliminals and therapy responded significantly better than the group receiving therapy only. Budzynski applied for a federal grant to study further the role of specific suggestions in subliminal scripts.

Behavior modification therapy is one of the most important uses of subliminals. Such therapy has been applied in areas as diverse as jet lag and agoraphobia. One interesting clinical approach, for example, was that taken by Dr. Dominic Marino. Treating a fifty-eight-year-old patient who feared thunderstorms, Marino used subliminal messages as part of a multifaceted means to alleviate the patient's maladaptive behavior associated with thunderstorms. Marino reported that the thunderstorm phobia was completely eliminated.

My own research has provided anecdotal evidence support-

ing the use of subliminal communication in such diverse applications as intervening in grand mal seizures to enhancing team
sports performance. As an example of the latter application,
Weber State College's football team went from one of their worst
losing seasons to win their conference championship in 1987,
after using subliminals as part of their training program, and the
National Judo Institute turned good athletes into world-class elite
performers. (See *Subliminal Learning*.) Clearly, subliminals can
relax us or prime us for action.

CHAPTER SIX

SUBLIMINAL TECHNOLOGY

Several ways exist to communicate subliminally. But perhaps, before we discuss various technical methods of communicating subliminally, it would be wise to differentiate the uses of the word *subliminal* and related words. *Subliminal* technically means any form of communication not consciously perceived. For our purposes here, the following definitions and distinctions of word usage and meaning apply:

Supraliminal is used to mean perceivable, although generally not perceived by the conscious mind. Associations, such as a politician and a baby, and contextual inferences, such as the inferences one draws from seeing the politician with the baby, are examples of supraliminal communication.

Subception refers to something ordinarily not perceivable by the conscious mind because of the operation of one or more defense mechanisms. An example would be a taboo embed, such as that used by *Playboy's* subscription ad and the wreath of genitalia discussed in Chapter 2.

Subliminal is that which *is not* assessed by the conscious mind because of some technical application that masks its accessibility, unless technical unmasking capabilities are first applied, or in rare instances of certain altered states of consciousness.

Supraliminal communication covers ordinary communication that may have unconscious communication inherent to it, and subception covers manipulation of the kind sometimes used by

32

advertisers in print media. Both of these forms of communication are accessible to the trained observer without the technical assistance of special equipment or instruments. It appears to me that legislating against them would seriously endanger our freedom of speech. In other words, we already have statutes regarding obscenity and pornography, and should an advertisement be deemed obscene or pornographic, jurisprudence is equipped to deal with it. (This might be a productive avenue in which to pursue some subliminal manipulators.)

Subliminal communication, then, refers to communication created with technical assistance (that is, with equipment, instruments, technology in general) that simply cannot be perceived directly by the conscious mind, irrespective of the observer's training or sophistication about such matters. For example, if a sound engineer back-masks a spoken message in a heavy-metal recording, creating a subliminal stimulus to the listener, the sound engineer does not possess the conscious ability to perceive the subliminal in the finished product any more than does any other listener without technical assistance from special instrumentation.

When these definitions and distinctions with respect to subliminal communication are understood, it should be easier to create legislation that does not infringe on constitutional rights and that would protect the public from subliminal exploitation.

Subliminal stimuli can be perceived at many sensory levels. Low-voltage electrical shock has been used to bring about responses when the voltage was too low for the recipient to have awareness of the shock conditioning. The neurophone developed by Dr. Patrick Flanagan has been demonstrated to electronically induce suggestions by skin contact. Dick Sutphen, a manufacturer of subliminals, claims that when this instrument was shown to the National Security Agency, it was promptly confiscated.

Literally every one of our senses can be appealed to subliminally, but the two most often addressed are the visual and the

33

audial senses. Generally, subliminal video stimuli are generated in one of three ways: slide insertion, candlepower ratio levels, or tachistoscope projection.

Slide insertion is essentially what was reportedly used in the theater houses in New Jersey. A slide may be inserted as often as one per fourteen frames and usually go consciously unnoticed. A simple visual method for understanding this technique can be produced with a fast-turn card deck, the kind children used to make. By inserting any message once every fourteen to twenty-eight frames and then by thumbing the deck rapidly, one can replicate the type of subliminal exposure involved in the slide insertion process.

Candlepower ratio levels are of the type discussed earlier with Dr. Ledford's erotica and violence. Simply lowering the wattage output or connecting a rheostat to a person's home projector to produce light slightly above that of the room will replicate this process. In fact, it might make for an interesting home experiment to use a slide projector to project a message such as "I like to study" behind the television set while the teenagers are glued to MTV.

Tachistoscope projection is accomplished by a device that flashes messages every five seconds at a speed of 1/3000th of a second. An ordinary projector with a high-speed shutter can be modified to produce this effect. Ordinarily, the candlepower method is more effective that the tachistoscope, simply because the message is continuous.

The tachistoscope itself was patented in 1967 (patent no. 3,060,795) by Precon Process and Equipment Corporation of New Orleans. According to Key in *Subliminal Seduction,* the device was originally used to flash subliminal messages on television and on theater screens. Key states that this was the method used by at least one theater during a six-week period to expose 45,699 patrons to the subliminals "Drink Coca-Cola" and "Hungry? Eat Popcorn." Key states that a survey research check conducted during July 1971 located thirteen commercial firms that (for the right price) could and would offer subliminal services to advertisers. What is more frightening, the survey targeted only three markets: New York, Chicago, and Toronto.

Audiosubliminals have created a new industry in America, selling instant fixes for everything from poverty to obesity. Many companies peddle absolute panaceas in their claims, implicitly if not explicitly. Some have adopted the "more is better" mentality, and there appears to be open competition over who can get the most affirmations on a single audiotape. In my opinion, not only is subliminal self-help here to stay but in the very near future it will be the preferred method for effecting beneficial change. Nevertheless, just as subliminals are *not* the invisible and therefore nonexistent-yet-pretended-to-be-perceived emperor's clothes, they are also *not* a panacea. There are definite limitations and even contraindications to their use. Be that as it may, however, it is the informed consumer who eventually will decide what companies remain in business when the initial awe of new technology is replaced by consumer awareness.

As with videosubliminal projection, a number of methods are involved in audiosubliminal projection. Perhaps the best known is the "black box," a device that Professor Becker patented in 1969, but there are at least three other very popular methods. Essentially, these methods are Becker's black box, psychoacoustical concealment, white-sound masking, and backmasking, or metacontrast. Several methods have been derived from each of these four, and there is some overlapping, as further discussion will reveal. In addition, there is great debate over the speed of messages as in time-compressed modalities and the frequency bands used to modulate the subliminal, especially where inexpensive players are used to review the content.

Becker's black box processes spoken words into music by simply averaging the volume levels of the music and producing the spoken word as a subliminal slightly beneath the music volume. Ordinarily, tracings of this process show the following:

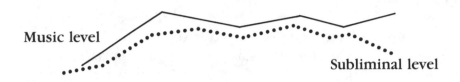

Because the process and its various derivations use averages, it is not at all uncommon to produce the following tracing:

It can be seen that the subliminal content may thus become audible or semiaudible during part of the programming.

Becker's process was tested in a supermarket in New Orleans during 1979. The black box mixed "Thou shalt not steal" and "Honesty is the best policy" into the Muzak system broadcast in the store. Reports of lowered cash shortages, inventory damage, and pilferage were astounding.

Becker's resourcefulness as both researcher and entrepreneur led to the creation of weight-loss programs that worked. Not only did the participants lose weight, but their losses were not regained. In 11 percent of the cases, the maintained weight loss was 25 percent; for 50 percent more, the maintained loss was 50 percent; and for the remaining 24 percent, the maintained loss was between 75 to 100 percent over a two-year period.

Becker's process has had numerous applications. It was used at McDonagh Medical Center and for the most part established the initial credibility of audiosubliminals.

A very close cousin to Becker's process is one developed by Dr. Louis Romberg. A native of East Germany, Romberg began researching subliminal communication in the early 1960s. Romberg's device was installed in a tire store in Toronto that offered a line of general hardware. Reportedly, employee productivity went up and thefts went down considerably.

According to *Subliminal Report* by Schroeder and Ostrander, some fifty retail store chains in the United States have introduced subliminals into their background music. It is assumed that the messages are antitheft messages such as "I am honest."

A second method of audiosubliminal projection is psychoacoustical concealment. Such concealment can be accomplished in a number of ways, one of which is to harmonize voice frequency with primary sound output. Sometimes the voice is made to sound like an instrument and sometimes like "pink" or "gray" sound, which is simply background sound such as the "swooshing" of a gentle wind.

A third method of audiosubliminal projection, white sound mixing, is in effect very nearly the same as psychoacoustical concealment. The difference is that white sound contains all audible sound frequencies. Therefore, the voice track used to produce the subliminal message either must be matched with the specific frequencies used by musical instruments or lowered slightly below the white sound background (usually the sound of ocean surf).

One company that reformats voice frequencies to conceal them in the music is Valley of the Sun. The creator of Valley of the Sun, Dick Sutphen, asserts that when efforts to acquire rights to Becker's black box were broken off, he engaged sound engineers in California to develop the process. Sutphen further states that the ease with which they came up with the process was frightening because, he says, this process conceals the subliminal content in such a way that it cannot be recovered, even by sophisticated equipment, including the parametric analyzer.

Anthony Pellicano declares that no such process exists. Pellicano founded Audio Forensic Laboratories in Los Angeles and for years has specialized in recovering voice content lost in background noises from audiotapes surreptitiously recorded by law enforcement agencies. Pellicano has the equipment and the technical expertise to separate the layers of audio content one layer at a time, almost like stripping an onion. If it's there, Pellicano says, it can be recovered.

This issue of recoverability is central to the Judas Priest case discussed in Chapter 1. Does a subliminal message in fact exist if it is not electronically recoverable? The answer is an emphatic no. If extremely sophisticated technology used in competent audio analysis, such as that performed by Audio Forensic Laboratories, shows that there is no recoverable verbal content under the music of a recording, then, regardless of what a sound engineer does in the original mixing, the stimuli are not sufficient to evoke a neuronal response in the listener.

Let's look at this issue another way. Imagine that you are in a concert hall listening to a symphony orchestra. In one passage the brasses totally overwhelm the softer strings. Even though you may not consciously perceive them, your subconscious is aware of the sounds made by the strings, which are registered on the electronic soundtrack of the symphony and can be separated—recovered—from the overpowering brasses by electronic equipment. Now imagine you are again in the same hall with the musicians playing the same passage of music as before. This time, however, we send the violinists a block away to continue playing. Not only is whatever they play no longer electronically recoverable from the soundtrack of the symphony, which is being recorded in the hall, but the sounds of the strings are not meaningful at all to the audience. In other words, the subaudible sound of the strings from a block away is insufficient to evoke a neouronal response in the listeners. So, in fact, an audiosubliminal is really an audioillusion.

A fourth popular method of audiosubliminal projection is back-masking, or metacontrast, which is usually accomplished in multiple track mixing. Here the audio track of spoken messages is reversed, or played backwards.

Ultrahigh and ultralow frequencies can also be incorporated

with any of these methods. The silent dog whistle is a simple example of a frequency not consciously perceived by the human ear and yet verifiably perceived by the human's unconscious or subconscious processes.

Sound engineer Glen Pace has had considerable personal experience with both high- and low-frequency mixing and back-masking. Pace was a recording engineering and record producer for about eighteen years and at one time was probably one of the top five recording engineers in Los Angeles. In a conversation in August 1986, he candidly discussed with me his experiences with subliminal communication, which began in the late sixties and early seventies when he was approached by some of the heavy-metal rock groups.

One of the objectives of heavy-metal recordings, according to Key in *Subliminal Seduction,* is to achieve popularity with the young people by appealing to their desire to torment adults, their parents in particular. Key further asserts that a manipulation of listeners' value norm anchor points was accomplished by injecting subaudible sounds, tones, and harmonics at levels that encouraged turning up the volume. Certain sounds, especially those recorded in the bass ranges, become audible by increasing the volume of the recording.

Pace was told that the idea for subliminal back-masking came from the East. Because the mind reverses what it perceives, the idea was to play backwards messages that the mind would then reverse. That idea is worth interrupting the continuity of our story for a moment.

The nature of our language is such that a single word often contains opposites. Think of the *sin* in *sincere* or remember the *con* in *confidence.* Then there are such words as those Marshall McLacken cites in the introduction to *Subliminal Seduction,* such words as *eros* and *live.* When these words are reversed, their meanings are drastically changed. *Eros* becomes *sore* and *live* becomes *evil.* It therefore is valid to ask whether or not heavy-metal groups using satanic subliminals are corrupting or evangelizing their audiences.

One question often asked about subliminal messages allegedly contained on certain popular music recordings is, Can they produce harmful effects? In other words, can messages like "kill your-self—your're no good—do it now!" result in self-destructive be-havior?

A study now underway tests the hypothesis that such messages absolutely can result in self-destructive behavior. No scientific study of this point has yet been completed. So, until the current study is concluded, we can offer only an opinion.

My opinion is probably very obvious. The primal child—you and I, in other words—sublimates primitive drives that are ter-ritorial, hostile, and aggressive and substitutes fight/flight with modern man's adaptation: anxiety/depression. These responses are wired into our autonomic nervous system. Still, lurking in the psyche, sometimes deep in the unconscious, are basal instincts dampened by "socially acceptable" enculturation. These basal instincts, when warmed by priming effects, can ignite or explode. Theoretically, therefore, temporary rage equal to that of any other predator in nature, can seize our functional rationality and, for all intents and purposes, turn off higher functions. Temporary rage can actually shut down, if you will, cortex inhibition. When that happens, nearly anything is possible.

Pace believes that he was one of the first few engineers to be involved in the "backwards thing." He said that he heard the groups discuss research from the Far East but never actually saw any of it. He told me further that in "a few years of watching it, knowing about it, it definitely had some merit to it." Some of the messages were picked up by the kids, and "you could see it in their behavior and they would have had no other way of depicting what we put on there." Pace says that the messages included all kinds of things, "everything from 'drugs are great' to satanic types of things." That is where he drew the line and refused to be involved any longer. He knows of two or three other engineers who did get involved in recording satanic messages for three of today's most popular rock groups. Originally, the back-masking was recorded on a monaural track or on two tracks, turned around, and blended in.

Pace stated to me that at the time he first put subliminal mes-sages on recordings, he couldn't have cared less about what they were doing—all he cared about was that they paid his bill. That

40

is not at all where Glen Pace stands today. A deeply religious man, he is committed to using subliminal technology for the benefit of mankind.

An electronics engineer and I developed a subliminal process mixer that maintains exact levels between primary and secondary carriers of very close decibel levels. This processor has other nuances to it and is used by Progressive Awareness Research. It delivers both a back-masked channel (left ear to right brain) and a forward-speech channel (right ear to left brain), a method and apparatus that are patent pending.

There are many other twists to the modalities outlined here, but some of the techniques either are considered trade secrets or are patented processes. In short, the means to create audiosubliminal recordings range from sophisticated digital recording equipment to the "home-made" version explained in Chapter 9, with do-it-yourself instructions.

Still, when properly done, an audiosubliminal is an audioillusion — not, and I repeat, not a silent voice that cannot be discerned even with electronic means.

You can do a simple demonstration that I have done for various behavioral scientists in America and Europe that provides a "picture," if you will, of an audioillusion.

Record a voice track mixed with ocean sounds so that the voice is barely audible above the ocean. Start the ocean and two minutes later add the voice. Take this mix and add music by bringing the music in one minute after the beginning of the ocean. The mind hears the ocean followed by music. It then says, There are no voices here, so by the time the voice begins, the mind is busy with other stimuli. Remember when you do this, as long as you can hear the ocean you know the words are present.

CHAPTER SEVEN

SCIENTIFIC FINDINGS

An argument could be made for subliminals having been used for centuries—at least since the Asclepiad healing centers of ancient Greece, which used subliminal information in creating the setting for healing—but that is beyond the scope of this work. Rather, this chapter presents data drawn from contemporary studies of subliminal technology and perception. Two of the most notable researchers in this field are Dr. Norman Dixon, author of *Preconscious Processing,* a veritable text on the subject for professionals, and Dr. Lloyd Silverman of New York University.

Dixon has probably participated in more diverse explorations of subliminal stimuli than anyone else. His research has resulted in the formulation of certain generalizations, one of which is that consciousness is not the same as information processing. There are at least two systems of information processing, and the conscious is aware of only one of them. Furthermore, the preconscious processor, the unconscious, performs tasks that formerly were thought to be the province of the conscious. For example, information such as the meaning of new words can be processed and integrated with relevant data in the memory, and responses can then be elicited without stimuli ever circuiting conscious awareness. Dixon's work represents a compendium of the application of subliminal stimuli and implications ranging from the traditional views of stimuli registration to the more unorthodox parapsychological.

Dr. Lloyd Silverman has researched subliminals for more than twenty years and is heralded by some as the world's foremost academic researcher of subliminal communication. His work with symbiotic fantasies has been the source of a host of studies and articles. Sometimes referred to as the "oneness fantasy," suggestions such as "mommy and I are one" and "it's okay to do better than daddy" have been demonstrated to possess near-panacean potential. Everything from learning ability to dart-throwing skills have been improved as a result of exposure to these subliminal messages. That may seem difficult to believe, but a commonly held idea in psychology is that a merging fantasy (a symbiotic fantasy), generally with archetypes, will improve adaptive behavior. (For more information, see *Subliminal Learning.*)

Silverman first undertook research into subliminal communication as a path to understanding the unconscious. He began with the hypothesis that conflict originating in the unconscious as the result of opposing wishes gives rise to adaptive behavior. (All behavior is adaptive, even if by convention it appears to be maladaptive.) The more serious and unresolved the conflict, the more deviant the behavior. Silverman proceeded to test his hypothesis by using visually embedded "psychoactivating subliminals," as he termed them. The theory worked. Schizophrenic symptoms were exacerbated by approximately 70 percent.

Silverman's "mommy" message was first discussed in psychological journals as the result of its successful use in a weight-loss class. Then Dr. Silverman and an associate, Dr. Rose Bryant-Tuckett, applied the "mommy" subliminal to a group of emotionally handicapped youngsters in a New York school. It was an informed consent situation, but no one in the experimental group knew what the message was. The device for measuring results was the California Achievement Reading Test. Silverman and Tuckett included a control group in their experiment and used the tachistoscope to present the subliminal message "mommy and I are one." Significantly higher scores were achieved by the children who viewed the subliminal than by the control group. In addition, a number of "spillover" gains were associated with the test group. These gains ranged from improved behavior to improved class grades in arithmetic.

Not unlike the spillover gains of Silverman and Bryant-Tuckett's findings, Dr. Kenneth Parker of Queen's College, in an experiment designed to improve academic performance of law students, found that the magic "mommy" message improved academic performance in general. Also using a control group that received neutral messages, Parker demonstrated significant gains by the test group. Not only this, but after one month those who had received the subliminal message had higher retention of the learning-enhanced material.

Attempts by researchers to duplicate the efficacy of the "mommy" subliminal have been made using deviations of the symbiotic fantasy. Such messages as "Daddy and I are one" and "the professor and I are one" proved less effective than the magical "mommy" message.

Dr. Sima Ariam tested the "mommy" subliminal on students in Tel Aviv and discovered that its effect may be crosscultural. Ariam, a student of Silverman, produced findings similar to those produced by his mentor. The archetypal "mommy" apparently is not bound just to western culture.

Silverman suggests that, paradoxically, the fantasy of oneness with mommy is an archetypal experience with the "good mother of infancy" that produces self-sufficiency. Silverman is quoted by the *Newsletter Perspective* as believing that at least one good ideal in mental health is the ability to vacillate comfortably between union, or the oneness fantasy, and individuation. The key word in the "mommy" message has been shown to be *one*. The essential aspect of "mommy" power appears to come from the oneness metaphor.

In recent, yet unpublished findings by Dr. Thomas Budzynski and his wife, Lawrence Doche-Budzynski, doctoral candidate at the University of Paris, "mommy" power was incorporated with "daddy" messages to bring about statistically significant findings. Their experiment was conducted with Type A males. An assumption based on the work of Freidman and others that

Type A males possess low self-esteem was part of their working hypothesis. Using four statistical measurement scales (the Minnesota Multiphasic Personality Inventory, the Jenkins Attitude Survey, the Tennessee Self-Concept, and the Cooper Self-Esteem), pretesting and posttesting revealed significant increases in the subjects' self-esteem.

Unlike the earlier work of others, the Budzynskis used audiosubliminals. The messages "mommy and I are one," variations of "it's okay to do better than daddy," and "I am good" were spoken slowly and meaningfully and then masked beneath the gentle sounds of ocean waves. No fancy multitracking, time-compressing, or voice-frequency switching was involved. The experimenters had participants use the audiotape once a day for four weeks. Listening to the program involved approximately twenty minutes each day. The experiment was designed as a double blind study. After four weeks, testing clearly indicated beneficial gains by the participants receiving the subliminal messages. In addition, ninety days later a residual gain remained measurable.

In South Africa, Dr. T. F. Pettigrew presented subjects with subliminals based on brain lateralization experiments. Simultaneously, each eye of the subjects viewed different pictures. While one eye received the slide of a white face, the other was presented with a black face. This dichotic experiment had some interesting results. South Africans were able to assemble the two faces and perceive a face. Native Africans were unable to bring about fusion of the images and to see a face.

Dr. Budzynski's work in the area of dichotic audiosubliminals appeals to this hemispheric difference insofar as dominant and minor functions are concerned and perhaps works as well as it does in part because of "blocking" aspects of perception. (See Chapters 5 and 6.)

One claim about the "mommy" subliminal is that it loses its power if conscious awareness becomes attached to its use. It is argued that this result is due to the ability of the conscious mind to accept or reject input, a sort of mitigation by conscious awareness. Most of the evidence that suggests this con-

45

clusion derives from research with visually presented subliminal stimuli—pictures and words.

On the other hand, I have been involved in an audio subliminally presented program with different findings. Lee Liston and Charles McCusker at the Utah State Prison and I developed a subliminal script that incorporated the "mommy" subliminal, which participants read before using the subliminal audiocassette program. Liston, an official with the Utah Corrections Department, had obtained permission to conduct the research, subject to certain conditions and limitations. McCusker's background in statistical psychology and computerized psychometrics was employed for taking measurements before and after the experiment was carried out.

A double-blind experiment was devised, using a waiting control group, a placebo group, and a test group. Two psychological measurement instruments, the Minnesota Multiphasic Personality Inventory and the Thurstone Temperament Scale, were incorporated for preevaluations and postevaluations. (See Appendix E.)

Pretesting showed three areas that were generally reflected by the inmates: low reflectivity scores, low sociability scores, and high self-alienation scores. Those three areas determined the content of the subliminal script.

One of our discoveries led us to believe that at least one propensity functioning with this particular volunteer population of inmates (forty in all) was inherent in the way they acted upon "poor self-esteem." It was as if they had decided that their low self-worth was indicative of society's low worth. If they weren't worth anything, no one else was either!

Consequently, the subliminal messages were designed to raise their self-appraisals as well as their appraisals of society. The following affirmations thus became the subliminal content of our program:

I am calm.
I am relaxed.
I am in control.
I create my future.
I am self-responsible.

I am patient.
I am honest.
I am peaceful.
I am tranquil.
I forgive myself.
I forgive others.
I am positive.
I am responsible.
I am happy.
I am confident.
I am capable.
I can do anything.
I am one with the Divine.
Mommy and I are one.
Honesty is oneness.
I live in oneness.
I like myself.
I like others.
I respect myself.
I respect others.
I love all.
All is oneness.
I am at peace in oneness.

Two audiotapes were created, identical except that one did not contain subliminal content. The affirmations were spoken slowly and deliberately, with meaningful voice inflections. The recordings used two primary carriers: ocean sounds and piano music performed in a pantanic scale. The project was flawed both by unforeseen and unexpected circumstances as well as by some of the conditions and limitations imposed by the state correctional system. (A detailed analysis is available from Liston, and an abstract of findings written by McCusker appears in Appendix F.) Nevertheless, statistically meaningful data were assembled. Because of the success of the project, additional studies are presently under way.

Some of the findings suggest the following conclusions:

1. The test group did receive significant measurable gain in three specific areas messages were tailored to address.

2. There was a degeneration of certain variables relevant to social adjustment, problems with authority, and self-esteem in most observations, taken from both the placebo and the control groups, ostensibly indicating either frustration or the role of the incarceration environment. Either way, this result tends to make positive swings even more statistically significant.

3. Twice as many participants dropped out of the placebo group as dropped out of the test group. (This experiment was conducted strictly on a volunteer basis, right down to the daily checking out of tape and player. No incentives and no coercion techniques were applied.)

4. The perceived environmental erosion arising from the control and placebo groups suggested application within thirty days of release for highest efficacy.

The subliminal program was designed to interrupt and diminish recidivism. Since those statistics are primarily organized in two-year groupings, follow-up on this measurement will not be available for some time yet.

As a result of these investigations and innumerable others, subliminal communication has earned credibility with the informed. In fact, recent research seems to assume that subliminal communication has been proven to exist. For example, one recent study indicates that certain personality types integrate subliminally perceived suggestions more readily than do other types. Some researchers suggest a similarity between personality types already associated with subliminal perception as "high psi hitters" with subliminal perception. (The term *psi* is used by parapsychologists for the energy or phenomena present in paranormal occurrences.) In an article appearing in *The Journal of the American Society for Psychical Research,* investigator Gertrude R. Schmeidler compared ESP as a normal psychological ability with subliminal perception skills. Her correlation statistics indicate a favorable comparison in that scores on the one can predict scores on the other. This positive correlation between ESP skills and subliminal perception suggests that it may be possible to cluster personality types before researching the effects of subliminal stimuli in order to examine relative differences between groups.

For further readings about the science of subliminal communication, see Recommended Readings (p. 101), especially *Subliminal Learning*, by Eldon Taylor, *Handbook of Psychology*, edited by Benjamin Wolman, and *Preconscious Processing*, by Norman Dixon.

CHAPTER EIGHT

UNANSWERED QUESTIONS

Despite the rather large body of research in the field of subliminal communication, there remain many more questions to be answered, not just for researchers but for consumers.

Ethical considerations are inextricably entwined with the issues of legislation and freedom of speech. There is also a question of competency versus freedom in the marketplace where commercial products such as self-improvement audio- and videosubliminals are concerned.

In addition, there is the old question regarding practicing psychology (or medicine) without a license. The entire inventory of Potentials Unlimited, the largest and one of the oldest manufacturers of subliminals for retail sale, was seized by United States marshals over allegations of practicing medicine without a license. Potentials Unlimited prevailed, but to some extent the issue remains unresolved.

Professor Key believes subliminals are potentially dangerous because they reach directly our deepest reservoirs of behavioral and belief systems. Add to this concern the fact that some companies produce videosubliminals that are dramas, in contrast to videosubliminals that typically feature beautiful nature scenes, and another dimension of concern enters the picture. One such video that I have seen (a very good one, in my opinion) is a psychodrama portraying an actress in a weight-loss motivation scenario. This video is manufactured and distributed by Valley of the Sun, but even its superior content in the cognitively observable drama could be argued to have "practicing psychology" implications. Yet in a very real sense, all entertainment appeals to and persuades, at some level, the psyche of each one of us. From entertainment our archvillains and heroes are spawned, our tolerances and intolerances as a society are shifted, and so forth.

Once again, I repeat my opinion that the final word on both availability and ethical considerations is and should be consumer based. But the covert application of subliminal technology is another matter. Although there are not yet any documented cases of injury or harm from subliminal programming, the literature certainly suggests the possibility for such harm exists. The well-known increase in teenage crime accompanied by satanic rituals, symbology, and suicide notes, and the like are just one area of concern. Only an informed and concerned public can help to encourage legislators to address this issue.

Fortunately, the overwhelming majority of researchers and commercial manufacturers openly working with subliminal communication are ethical. Yet there appears to be a sort of "Catch 22" here. If those openly working with subliminals are ethical, then laws are needed to protect us from hidden messages employed by secret producers. How, then, do we discover the hidden messages and pursue the secret producers? Obviously, herein lies another problem: either everything is policed carefully for subliminals or paranoia regarding "hidden persuaders" prevails. The issue is complex, but ignoring it will not cause it to go away.

If television is used to project subliminal messages, the Orwellian possibilities are even greater. According to Dick Sutphen, in a transcript from his taped program *The Battle for Your Mind,* Dr. Herbert Krugman has shown that viewers of television demonstrate more right-brain activity than left by a ratio of two to one. For most, using the right brain results in the chemical release of certain natural opiates (encephalins and beta-endorphins). The result is simply that the person feels good. The intrigue deepens when we combine this finding with the observation of Dr. Thomas Mulholland, a psychophysiologist

51

in Bedford, Massachusetts, who discovered that children's brain-wave patterns are predominantly alpha waves when viewing television and that the majority of those tested were unable to maintain a predominance of ordinary beta waves even when instructed to concentrate. Predominant alpha waves signify right-brain activity, which, as we have said, is associated with the body's release of natural opiates.

Now, add the "black slide" or "black frame" technique, whereby every thirty-second frame in a film being projected is black, thus producing forty-five-beat-per-minute pulsations perceived only at a subconscious level, and we have trance induction. In that case, any suggestion, subliminal or otherwise, is much more likely to be acted upon by the viewer.

It is worth noting that speeding up the standard twenty-four frames per second (FPS) to sixty FPS increases physiological stimulation. In fact, at least one special-effects expert, Douglas Trumball, has tinkered with this concept and refined it into a process he calls Showscan. In addition to increasing excitement, Showscan is said to stimulate feelings of voyeurism and to facilitate enhanced recall. The possibility of misusing this technique where subliminal input is involved is frightening. On the other hand, using Showscan in an accelerated learning situation is exciting.

Still others view subliminal messages as the work of the devil, messing with the mind, un-Christian, and so forth. As a cleric myself, I personally find this perspective ignorant and unwarranted. The mind is influenced by all of life's various stimuli. Life and stimuli are significant experiences having to do with this physical dimension. The nature of the physical world is what Heracleitus termed "constant flux." The flux is between energy and matter, as the Einsteinian equation demonstrates. There is no such thing as energy or matter that is inherently evil. Evil is given rise to by the use (or misuse) of energy and matter.

Subliminal communication has as many possibilities for positive applications as it has possibilities for subversive use. It is not the technology itself but the people behind the application of the technology that should be examined for motive and intent—good or evil. For example, I am aware of one Christian group that is considering subliminal audiotapes as a potential proselyting tool. To any conscientious observer concerned with individual rights, freedom of religion, or the integrity of America's Bill of Rights, this is almost as alarming as satanic messages in heavy-metal recordings.

Another interesting question that presently is the focus of much research is the nature of the subliminal voice track. Should the voice track be multitracked, multifrequencied, sped up (as in the process known as time compression), or said slowly, methodically, with contextual reference?

Some manufacturers, as mentioned earlier, are apparently of a "more is better" mentality. I have heard claims that at least one manufacturer produced sixty-minute cassette subliminal recordings with more than a million affirmations on each. In my opinion this is one of several absolutely outrageous claims made by sellers competing with other sellers for consumer dollars. With sufficient propaganda, some companies are selling products comparable to those made by others less inclined to aggressive marketing and exaggeration for three or four times the less aggressive competitor's retail price.

In order to get a million affirmations on a tape sixty minutes long, the affirmations must be multitracked and time compressed. When the human voice is sped up to fifteen and even more times the natural speed of delivery, it is questionable whether the resulting communication is any more meaningful than electromagnetic smog. In my opinion, and in the opinion of many other independent researchers, this procedure is unmitigated nonsense. (See *Subliminal Learning.*)

If you remember the Chipmunks for a minute, you can easily construct some sort of neutral image of what goes on in time compression. Speeding up the human voice from two to three times will produce the Chipmunk sound. It is difficult to imagine the Chipmunks saying anything that is taken seriously, but now speed that up five to seven more times, and the conscious mind simply observes noise.

Dr. Steven Halpern states that the United States government is presently looking into evidence that links sound pollution to physiological dysfunction and electromagnetic smog to molecular mutations. Halpern, an authority on sound and music as it affects the human condition, further suggests that unheard sounds—vibrations—are perhaps as important to our environment as any of those perceived. Maybe that is stretching just a little bit my concern regarding subaudible messages time compressed and multitracked and even multifrequencied—but perhaps more research will tell.

Meanwhile, there is another and even more credible concern. Simply stated, if the conscious mind can make absolutely no sense out of messages audibly presented at such speeds, what on earth leads anyone to believe that the subconscious could make sense of them? Science is well aware that the subconscious perceives many times more stimuli than that which is available to conscious awareness. Nevertheless, there exists no scientific proof that the subconscious makes meaningful recordings out of any input that is unintelligible. In fact, the overwhelming consensus of opinion from both practicing professionals and the published literature suggests that a subliminal verbal communication should be delivered slowly and methodically. Recall the Budzynski double blind study and the Utah State Prison double blind study reported in the last chapter; both studies used real-time verbal subliminals. Dr. Betty Randolph of Success Center is emphatic about "sink time." Randolph told me that all of her tapes allow fifteen-second "sinks" in the subliminal audio track to rest the brain, so to speak. In a recent conversation, Dick Sutphen stated that he had just written an article for publication effectively asserting that fifteen-to-one time compression was no more meaningful to the subconscious mind than the whine the conscious mind would hear if the messages were played without the subliminal masking.

Language is contextual, full of inference and expression values. One can use profanity in a humorous manner or in a manner that provokes an angry response. The method of delivery very often implies the meaning. Subliminal verbalizations, in my opinion, should be intoned seriously and spoken slowly and meaningfully. If multitracked, they should be recorded in a sequential, "round-robin" manner.

Back-masking could have its advantages. Some studies suggest that back-masked messages are received primarily by the right hemisphere of the brain, thereby appealing more directly to the emotional side of a person's being and behavior.

The subconscious mind is not concerned with sentences. A process known as subconscious cerebration takes place when words are put into the subconscious mind. Like a dice tumbler in Las Vegas, the subconscious just tumbles words around. Words become separated from each other in their original sentence structure. For this reason, it is absolutely critical that all affirmations used in subliminal communication be positively directed at the change designed to be brought about. For example, a tapering-off smoking script that said, "I find ten cigarettes a day more than enough for me," may tumble around and become "more than ten cigarettes."

It is also important that *no* aversive approaches be included. Since a known deterioration effect to the subliminal may follow its suspended use and the result may be that the nonsmoker starts smoking again, it is irresponsible to leave associations about black lungs and smoking in the subconscious, for this creates a psychological predisposition or expectation of lung disease. Aversive therapy was by and large abandoned a decade ago, in large part because of this type of backlash. As with the iatrogenic effect physicians are careful of, affirmations linking negatives to the stated objective may bring about more negative results than the desired positive ones.

Subliminal verbalizations should also be first person, such as "I this" and "I that," or egoless. Some research suggests that positive words alone can elicit associations that produce emotions related to the associations and thereby transform a negative state of mind into a positive one. (See *Megabrain,* by Michael Hutchison.)

Another nuance to language is the manner in which we take in information. For example, some of us are primarily visual and therefore "see" information. We see the problem or we see what someone else means ("I see what you mean"). Others of us are kinesthetic, or feeling oriented. We *feel* instead of *see.*

Many differences between people can be reduced to arguments over and between "I feel this way . . . " responded to by "Well, I see it this way . . . " So to some, visual phrasing is more powerful than tactile or auditory, for example. Language in a subliminal script should take these differences into consideration to create vivid, sensory information.

Because the verbal content of subliminals offered in the marketplace is of such great importance, I lean to the companies that disclose their content. With the possible exception of the symbiotic message, there is no evidence to indicate advantage in "unknown" content over consciously reviewed content. Remember that the inmates participating in the Utah State Prison study reviewed consciously the entire script, including the symbiotic message.

It seems appropriate for a consumer to expect a subliminal program to contain the two symbiotic phrases:
1. Mommy and I are one. 2. It's okay to do better than daddy.

It seems equally rational that a manufacturer would omit printing these two affirmations in the list of verbal statements. Perhaps in this way the best of both worlds could be achieved.

I believe that an equally appropriate set of phrases should be included with the two symbiotic phrases in subliminal programs. This set is what I call "the forgiveness set." My research has clearly demonstrated the efficacy of the forgiveness principle, which consists of three statements:
1. I forgive myself. 2. I forgive all others. 3. I am forgiven.

Like the symbiotic statements, "the forgiveness set," used alone, has produced some incredible clinical results. (See *Subliminal Learning* for more information.)

Another concern regarding verbalizations has nothing to do with the script but rather with the sex of the voice communicating subliminally. Some research indicates that certain personality types will respond to one or the other (male or female) in a preferential manner.

Dr. Thomas Budzynski indicated in a telephone conversation that certain feminists had experienced reverse effects from his weight-loss program. That is to say, they went on an eating binge for a few days, but the effects were not lasting, other than the women involved ceased using their subliminal audiotapes. Budzynski attributes this response to the male voice and the strong resentment held by certain female subjects for male authority figures.

It seems obvious that if consumers have a problem with a particular self-help title, perhaps they should investigate the voice behind the audible and try a voice of the opposite sex before abandoning the technology. We may well see in the future sex-voice alternatives as a regular part of the commercial menu.

Dr. Betty Randolph, creator of the Success Center tapes, uses both male and female voices on most of her titles, as does Gateways, an Ohai, California, manufacturer. Audio Activation offers a choice of male or female voice for each of their programs, and Progressive Awareness Research uses male, female, and child voices on all of their programs. Sound engineer Lance Cosgrove uses male and female voices, channeling the male voice to the left brain and the female voice to the right. All other companies I am aware of use either a male voice or a female voice.

Another alternative for consumers to consider is the dichotic, or "whole-brain," programming. For more than ten years, Dr. Thomas Budzynski has incorporated a combination of Twilight Learning (brain biofeedback) with nondirective hypnosis in therapeutic settings. He combined this learning with findings from his work in brain lateralization—a different subliminal message to each hemisphere. The result is a dichotic subliminal program that presents numbers the listener is supposed to repeat out loud to distract the major, or dominant, hemisphere so the minor, or less dominant, hemisphere will receive the information free of censorship or argument.

It is generally held that for most right-handers, the major hemisphere is the "left brain" and the minor hemisphere, the "right brain." The left brain, then, is usually the discriminate brain; the right brain is the indiscriminate. The left is the analytical; the right is the creative; and so forth. It is also generally accepted that the minor hemisphere processes more deeply emotional content and is the repository for unconscious motives behind habits, beliefs, and attitudes.

57

Dr. Budzynski's hypnotic subliminals incorporate permissive language, such as "It's okay to feel good," directed at the major hemisphere, and more authoritarian statements, such as "I do feel good," directed at the minor hemisphere. These lateralized messages are delivered through earphones. In the case of the typical right-hander, the permissive and audible message enters the right ear to travel to the left brain while the authoritarian subliminal travels from the left ear to the right brain.

Progressive Awareness Research produces programs similar to Budzynski's, except that PAR's products deliver the authoritarian statement in metacontrast to eliminate the need for earphones. The assumption is that because of the task orientation of major and minor hemispheres, the right hemisphere will process the back-masked affirmations while the left hemisphere is processing the forward statements.

A highly analytical person may want to try the strict dichotic approach if headphones and time out for concentrated effort are practical. On the other hand, my own research leans toward subliminal input that is hemispherically tasked according to the primary functions of each hemisphere's participation in language. This way, a person could use headphones for clear channel separation or play the program without headphones to allow for the brain's natural task differentiation to occur.

Still another area to be considered from the perspective of both researcher and consumer is the primary carrier of the subliminal (music, nature sounds, etc.). Much new research has recently confirmed the age-old adage that "music calms the savage breast"—at least certain types of music do.

Dr. Steven Halpern is one of the leaders in a field often referred to as "new age" music. Halpern's music has been fieldtested and demonstrated to relieve anxiety and tension levels, increase learning skills, raise pain thresholds, and more. In his book *Sound Health,* Halpern asserts that music is routinely used in the Soviet Union to raise pain thresholds and thereby minimize the use of pharmaceuticals.

A major difference between new age music and popular music is that in new age music the rhythm is not stop-antipaestic, meaning simply that there is no beginning, middle, or end. A

person can listen to this music over and over and still be unable
to hum along or anticipate the movement.

Another leading musician in this area is Jim Oliver. Oliver
has worked with medical professionals for years, measuring
major and minor muscle groupings and their responses to different notes, wave frequency forms (square wave, sine wave,
etc.), duration of intonation, and so forth. In a telephone conversation, he reported work with health professionals that was
absolutely astounding. (A paper on their findings is anticipated
in the near future.) He calls the study of music in connection
with psychological and physiological responses *symphonics.* It
is known elsewhere as bioacoustics or body acoustics. (See
Subliminal Learning for further information.)

Sheila Ostrander and Lynn Schroeder, authors of
Superlearning, a must on anyone's reading list, document the
use of baroque music as an essential aspect of the superlearning process. They go to great lengths, listing various classical
pieces that produce the desired effects.

Baroque music, usually largo in speed of performance, seems
to give rise to mind entrainment, thereby slowing down brain-
wave patterns. This slowing down enhances the learning process. The slowed-down brain-wave patterns combine with timed
repetition of material to produce incredible increases in learning. Repetitive material delivered in this manner is reminiscent
of the therapeutic repetition of suggestions in hypnosis. For
that matter, the same sort of repetition takes place in the media.
As Dr. Roy Udolf points out, the repetition of a message with
perhaps a slight change, such as an omission of the concluding
portion of an often-viewed ad, is especially effective. Perhaps
one reason for the effectiveness is the "zeigarnik" effect, which
is produced by the omission of the closure expected by the
audience.

Advertisers and the entertainment industry have long appre-
ciated the effect music has on the viewer. Among other things,
music can excite us, motivate us, raise deep emotion, and build
terror. According to Manfred Clynes, studies clearly suggest
that basic neurological forms, or patterns, correspond to emotional sets. Clynes refers to this correspondence as "sentics"

("essentic forms"). Using a computer to play standard notes directly proportional to the intensity and duration associated with different emotions, Clynes discovered that listeners experienced the emotion.

Perhaps some clarification of Clynes's method is warranted. Clynes originally observed and recorded finger pressure applied by volunteers to pressure-sensitive instruments. The participants were asked to express differing emotions in this manner. The conclusion Clynes drew was that the "touch" of music is more emotionally meaningful than the rhythm or the pitch. Drawing on this research, Clynes began to look carefully at the "shape" of emotions, or "sentics." He found that only minimal variations, as slight as 2 percent in the duration or amplitude of notes, were critical to whether a musical piece was perceived as extremely moving or merely routine.

Not only do we feel music but with the aid of technology we can examine visual representations of it. "Cymatics," as this field is called, evidences in natural geometry the amazing truth that inorganic matter vibrated by sound produces organic patterns. In fact, we are at last coming to understand what Pythagoras treated as sacred geometry. Pythagoras, as every student of geometry knows, was the mathematician who propounded the Pythagorean theorem. But he was also a mystic. He added the sixth string to the lyre because, he flatly insisted, order grew out of order, and he taught that natural geometry was a representation of divine order.

Studies in cymatics have revealed some results that clearly bear out Pythagoras' teachings. The discoverer of cymatics, Dr. Hans Jenny, demonstrated that wave patterns generated by music and sound can be visually displayed. Jenny, working largely from the findings of physicist Ernest Ehladni, discovered that liquids, powders, and metal filings scattered on a disc were moved into geometric patterns by the resonating of the disc to musical notes. These patterns became more than geometry ordered by mathematics. The new patterns took on the same assemblage as organic shapes. With a tonoscope, a device that converts sounds issued into a microphone into their corresponding visual configurations, some interesting representations

60

become perceivable. Some music creates the geometry of nature; in fact, much of it replicates the geometry of organisms. The mantra *om,* according to Jenny, always produces a perfect circle filled with concentric squares and triangles:

The concluding chord of Handel's *Messiah* produces a perfect, five-pointed star:

Other music, some heavy-metal recordings, for instance, produce discordant, or unnatural, geometry, much as a child scribbles on a piece of paper with no picture in mind. Perhaps this discordant geometry is visible evidence of why, when continually exposed to certain heavy-metal recordings, cows give little milk, chickens stop laying, and rats, normally conjugal creatures who mate once and then rear their young, suddenly become adulterers and devour their offspring.

The efficacy and the advantage of synchronized words and music in subliminal communication is clearly demonstrated by Colin Rose in a comparison of brain tomographs in his work *Accelerated Learning.* The tomograph, developed by Professor

61

Michael Phelps of the University of California at Los Angeles, essentially operates by using radioactive chemicals and a scanner to identify the chemicals and the brain's active areas.

The music is important esthetically to the consumer as well. Usually a consumer begins with one or two titles and literally builds a library of subliminal programs. Three companies manufacturing audiosubliminals match the subliminal script with music designed specifically to enhance the desired objective (that is, memory skills are paired with baroque music, and so forth). Superlearning, a company created by Ostrander and Schroeder, Halpern Sound, and Whole Brain Body Acoustics, by Progressive Awareness Research, select certain music tracks to accompany their individual titles and increase their efficacy. Subliminal programs created in this way are the more expensive ones. Two other companies offer a choice of music for each of their titles, and although the music is not necessarily selected to enhance the subliminal property, it nevertheless provides variety.

Although it is possible to enhance one with the other, it is the subliminal, not the music, that is at work in these programs. In fact, Dr. Steven Halpern reported conducting an experiment on just this point. He recorded a sleep and a wakefulness tape with identical music. Those who listened to the programs responded according to their content, or, as the titles suggest, one group became sleepy while the other stayed awake.

Nevertheless, music does play a significant role in psychophysical response—stimulating or relaxing, enhancing learning, evoking emotions, producing balance or discordance, and a wide range of other reactions. Different beats will produce different results. Advertisers, for example, have learned that a pattern of seventy-two beats per minute increases suggestibility. Key suggests, further, that seventy-two beats per minute voice, drum, and music appear to suggest the listener right into the symptoms a product is purported to cure (a headache).

A large body of classical music lends itself naturally to the production of certain effects in the human animal. According to one French researcher, Mozart pieces played frequently improve health. Mme. Belanger asserts that breathing, cardio-vascular, and brain-wave rhythms are coordinated, acting on the unconscious to stimulate perception and receptivity. Steven Cooter, educational theorist, has monitored his own brain-wave patterns via EEG instrumentation while listening to baroque rhythms. At sixty beats per minute, Cooter discovered that a complete and balanced pattern emerged; that is, proportion-ally balanced beta, alpha, and theta waves were displayed. Baroque music, usually by Vivaldi, Bach, Handel, Telemann, or Corelli, are integral aspects of superlearning or accelerated learning programs.

Sound definitely shapes responses—responses that can have considerable effect on the human condition. One interesting observation I have made of the thousands of users who visit the Mind Mint stores is that there seems to exist a certain kind of condition-response learning that arises from the association of the music used to carry the subliminal. For example, a per-son who has used a title (perhaps a stress-free title) responds immediately to the sound of the music for some time after dis-continuing the use of the audiosubliminal program. This phe-nomenon would make an interesting subject of investigation as it appears to have ramifications that are somewhat disquieting.

Another form of music is nature's symphony. Something about the gentle sounds of ocean waves or a creek babbling in the background, with occasional bird sounds interspersed, produces a quieting, relaxed atmosphere. Some have asserted that the water sounds appeal to deeply rooted intrauterine experiences, implying that the sound is reminiscent of an earlier sanctuary in the womb. And perhaps this is especially appealing to the child in all of us, an archetypal communication resulting in the production of secure, warm feelings. Several manufacturers of audiosubliminal programs integrate nature sounds in their soundtracks.

As indicated earlier, there are several possible reasons for resistance to subliminals, which may occasionally occur. The reasons are as diverse as resistance to the sex of the voice to resistance to an unknown script. Generally, where the "unknown" is concerned, simply reviewing consciously the verbalization will either assuage the anxiety or cause it to surface. A resistance to a voice is overcome by simply changing the sex of the voice. But there can be many other complex reasons for resistance, and though most resistances are simply feelings of discomfort that are resolved with repeated use of the subliminal program, nevertheless, I am of the opinion that use should be discontinued if the resistance persists for more than twenty repetitions of the title.

Should some self-destructive behavior appear, I suggest not only cessation of the use but also consultation with an appropriate professional. Subliminals are *not* a replacement for professional health care, and although many professionals use them, they are used to facilitate or augment beneficial gains in an ancillary way. Subliminals are not quick fixes, but their use is doubly appealing, principally because they are extremely affordable and require very little effort to use or to produce the gains desired. The use of subliminals by individuals under professional care is entirely dependent upon the health care professional.

Literature dealing with subliminals and schizophrenics suggests controversial findings. One patient of an associate of Budzynski's reported relief as a result of using a subliminal cassette; however, the relief, together with the willingness to play the tape, sharply ended when the patient was shown the subliminal script (it included a symbiotic fantasy) at the patient's insistence. Budzynski told me that this was not an unexpected outcome, given the history of this patient.

A more common resistance is one that is tied to choices. All behavior is the result of choices—some are consciously adopted, but most are made at an unconscious level. For instance, I once used a stop-smoking subliminal program. After about ten days, it occurred to me one morning that my cigarettes tasted nasty and, what was worse, the smell was nauseating. Instead of choosing to stop smoking at that time, I *chose* to stop playing the subliminal cassette.

Budzynski related a somewhat comparable story in a phone conversation. He recalled using a subliminal experiment that contained an aversive verbalization. The subliminal might have made the user sick, but it did not stop the smoking.

All in all, however, there is absolutely no documented evidence of subliminal self-help programs producing harm. Even the old argument of symptom substitution does not apply. As Ostrander and Schroeder succintly point out in their *Subliminal Report,* where subliminals are concerned, one need not experience a restriction in one area because of a gain in another.

Positive suggestion is as old as history itself. The principal difference where subliminal communication is concerned is that the conscious mind cannot argue and thereby influence or erode the efficacy of the suggestion's content. It is as simple as a scenario in which one is told that he feels great and he responds, as we all might, with "Well, maybe" or "No, I don't." The positive suggestion has been filtered, influenced, and interpreted by the cognitive process.

More than ever the words "you are what you think you are" echo with meaning. Subliminal communication can facilitate the "think" that is laden with self-doubt and limitation into an acceptance of "I *know* I am good!"

Still other unanswered questions deal with technical aspects of production. Since this work is not intended to be a sound engineer's supplement, I will be extremely brief. First, if digital recording is employed, what clock rates or vibrating frequencies are preferred as carriers for subliminal scripts? Second, is digital preferred to analog? Third, at what decibel level does communication perceived subliminally cease to be perceivable? In the years to come I am certain that most, if not all, of these areas will be fully investigated.

Another area of research that I am interested in, although I hesitate to mention it, is that of intentionality. I'll back up a little in order to explain. Our quantum physicists inform us that everything ultimately is wave form in a sea of electromagnetic energy. The "M-field Theory" further suggests not only that there is a connective circle between thought and wave form but also that thought can be and is influenced by some interaction occurring at an unseen level—in the wave form.

65

The "M-field Theory" is based on evidence that learning a subject, any subject—Morse Code, for example—occurs more rapidly when the subject matter has been previously learned by other groups or individuals. The more learning that has occurred or taken place with a subject, the more easily a new individual or group learns it. It is directly proportional, one to the other. Jung's collective unconscious revisited?

Is there such a thing as field psychology? Something like field physics? In other words, can we register nonverbal stimuli? I think so. One of my own experiments was designed to test this hypothesis. Two identical rooms were created. One was the "good" room, and the other was the "bad" room. Every day the "good" room received praise and wonderful thoughts and shared in meditative moments and spiritual fullness; every day the "bad" room received all the negative abuse imaginable—acts or thoughts or words alone. Did this create a field? If electrophotography is an indicator, the answer is yes. The "bad" room contracted the bioplasma (aura) of the subject, the colors became dull, and the geometry became discordant. Conversely, the "good" room produced brightened fields alive in color and organic in their geometry.

You can try this experiment yourself. Take two beans and plant them under identical conditions in two separate pots. Label one "love" and the other "hate." Each evening shower "love" with affectionate and loving superlatives full of as much emotion as you can express sincerely. Each evening dump all of your ill feelings on "hate." Treat it as though it were the ugliest creation, the most hated person or situation you can imagine. Let go of all your negative feelings and thoughts onto "hate." Express all of your higher and loving feelings toward "love." At the end of sixty days, you will witness marked differences in the two bean plants. Now, is this verbal or emotional content that the plants are responding to? Is it the power of thought behind the expression? Is it both, and perhaps more?

It is my opinion that electromagnetic processes, including the simple ones involved in manufacturing cassette tapes—the magnetic encoding of sound-wave transmissions—are equally applicable to thought transmissions. In short, I believe that "intentionality" could influence the subliminal efficacy of any experiment. The question I have is a simple one. Could intentionality alone be perceived and acted upon through the modality of subliminal input? In other words, could *thought* be transferred as *thought* through magnetic media? I think so. It would make for an interesting experiment, to say the least. I am aware of one subliminal manufacturer that blesses their master recordings just as the cleric blesses holy water. (For more on this intriguing subject of information processing, see the holographic model of perception in "wholes" developed in *Subliminal Learning.*)

Finally, there are some frequently asked consumer-related questions about self-help subliminals:

Q: Can more than one program be used at a time without disadvantage?

A: Yes, provided that no two programs undertake major behavioral modification. For example, one would not want to attempt cessation of drug abuse and weight loss at the same time. Most of the literature suggests that compatible titles such as memory improvement and good study habits would enhance one another. Using unrelated titles that are not threatening to one's basic drive mechanisms, such as removal of warts and taking examinations, is just as efficient as using only one.

Q: How often should the tapes by used?

A: You *cannot* overdose on positive suggestions. Many users have reported incredible results when automatic reverse players have been employed to continuously expose them for several days to a subliminal program. Nearly all manufacturers guarantee their products on the basis of recommended usage that consists of listening to the program once a day for thirty days.

Q: Is there a best time to listen to the tapes?

A: One can use the tapes as background while involved in any activity. No deliberate listening intensity is required. Users have reported excellent results using subliminal programs at bedtime, during drive times, and even while watching television. Again, no conscious effort is involved.

Q: How do I know that what I'm getting is actually the message the manufacturer says is on the tape?

67

A: By purchasing from major manufacturers that disclose their subliminal content, the old law of the dollar rules. To risk an entire profitable business by covertly "messing" with the stated scripts simply does not make any sense. It is easy with the right technology to "take apart" and examine the content on most tapes. Some tapes can be examined by using earphones with separate volume controls. Tuning into either left or right channel only is all that is necessary for the verbal to become audible or at least semiaudible.

Q: How soon can I expect results from using a subliminal tape?

A: Most people sense beneficial results within a week or two. All should be aware of gains or adverse reactions within sixty days if the program is solidly conceived and produced.

Q: Who uses subliminal programs?

A: Everyone from health professionals to educators. Many athletic programs, sales organizations, government agencies, retailers, and others use subliminals, to say nothing of the millions of individual users.

Q: Can I use the programs while I sleep?

A: One recommended way is to use an autoreverse player going all night long while you sleep. Although sleep learning, deep theta brain wave sleep, is still controversial, at least the REM cycles accompanying dream sleep and the hypnogogic and hypnopopic stages entering and exiting sleep (alpha brain wave sleep) are extremely susceptible periods for positive programming.

Q: Do I need to keep using the programs for the rest of my life?

A: Maybe yes—maybe no. That really depends on you. A subliminal is only a positive information antidote for negative messaging. When the negative ceases to exist, the antidote is no longer necessary.

CHAPTER NINE

THE HOMEMADE SUBLIMINAL PROGRAM

Creating an audiocassette subliminal program that works is a relatively simple process, although perhaps too expensive to prove practical. The procedure outlined in this chapter was used in my own early research. This process will *not* produce commercial quality audio mastering, but it will provide a usable product. In fact, it was this process that was used to create the subliminal titled "A Gift of Love" that is used in Utah by Sunrise, a support group for survivors of suicide victims. Testimonial evidence suggests that it works very well.

There are certain advantages to creating your own subliminal property. You should weigh those advantages against professional standards and quality before investing the time or money necessary to produce a personalized subliminal program.

Some of the obvious advantages include a subliminal script that can be uniquely and precisely what you desire. (Be careful here—much bad karma will come from deliberate or exploitive misuse.) Also, you can select whatever music or principal sound carrier you prefer. You may choose the gentle sounds of a waterfall or ocean background while viewing television. I am reminded here of a woman who played surreptitiously to her teenagers a good study habits program produced by Success Center and carried by ocean waves while they viewed television. She reported that within a short time the teenagers turned off the television set and moved to their rooms to study.

Whatever the primary carrier, be careful of copyright infringements!

Another advantage is that the voice on the subliminal track can be your own. There is much research suggesting that one responds advantageously to his or her own voice in many circumstances.

The six steps to creating a custom program are these:
1. Select and obtain the equipment.
2. Write and record the script.
3. Record the white sound.
4. Mix the script recording with the white-sound recording.
5. Select the principal carrier.
6. Mix the product of step 4 with the principal carrier.

Select and obtain the equipment. The equipment needed consists of three cassette players, of which one must have recording and external input capability and the other two must be equipped with external output functions, a two- to four-channel sound mixer, and a white-sound generator. Inexpensive mixers are readily available from such places as Radio Shack.

White-sound units are available from a number of variety and hardware outlets. These units are simple and relatively inexpensive devices that generate the sounds of running water, ocean surf, etc. Or you can substitute a recording of the sounds of ocean surf for the white-sound unit.

You will also need at least four blank cassettes of the length of playing time you choose.

Write and record the script. Write your affirmations in an all positive manner (see Chapter 8), then speak them slowly and meaningfully into one of the cassette recorders. Repeat the script over and over for the desired length of time. When finished, rewind the audio track now containing the verbalization.

Record the white sound. Now record another cassette with the chosen white sound, possibly ocean waves. This recording should be the same length as the audio-voice track; for example, thirty minutes.

Mix the script recording with the white-sound recording. Using the players with external output, connect the mixer (mono: two channels; stereo: four channels). Adjust the mixing volume so that you can barely perceive the spoken affirmations when they are mixed with the white sound. When all adjustments are made, record the mix using the recorder with external input for the desired length of the finished product.

Select the principal carrier. Select now the principal carrier. For your homemade version, music generally works best, although you can remix white sound with white sound. Place this cassette tape—and if it is not already a cassette tape, convert it into one—in the player that carried the voice recording.

Mix the product of step 4 with the principal carrier. Place the recorded product of your first mix in the player that formerly carried the white-sound-only recording, and mix your two recordings onto one new master.

Good luck, and remember the Golden Rule!

Before going to the time and expense involved in creating your own, you may want to inquire of one of the established companies distributing subliminal products. Many companies will provide custom subliminal work for substantially less than the cost of equipment to produce homemade tapes.

CHAPTER TEN

IN SUMMARY

Anyone who takes the time and makes the effort necessary to review the literature, conduct studies, and otherwise become fully involved at an interactive level with a subject deserves to have an opinion on that subject. Opinions are always relative to the contextual reference implied by "authority," but I am not sure there is any such thing as an authority on subliminal communication, even though there are some very good authorities on various aspects of it, for subliminal communication transcends boundaries inherent to disciplines. There is obviously no specialized discipline graduating students with degrees in "subliminal."

Subliminal communication for the most part is still in the investigative stages. Because this is true, most of those working with subliminal this and subliminal that view themselves as pioneers. In this pioneer's opinion, subliminal communication is one of the most promising means by which to explore dynamically the pragmatic power of the mind.

In the metaphor of Maxwell Maltx, many of us have become slaves to our unconscious computers. Our synthetic experiences are generally negative, and our expectations are almost invariably limiting. Our individual biocomputer, functioning as a servo-automechanism, is programming dismal realities despite our conscious kicking and struggling, perhaps because most of us were raised to believe we couldn't, wouldn't, and shouldn't—

shouldn't even try. As with any calculator when it is asked to compute, if there is more negative input than positive, the result is negative.

Subliminal communication offers an affordable and effortless way to rewrite and rebalance the language and equations existing in the biocomputer, that is, the unconscious or subconscious mind. Thus, through subliminal communication, we really have an opportunity to truly take charge of the controls. We can indeed change ourselves and the world around us. With this realization the possibilities become limitless.

Today you can be what you think you are, not what others thought you might be. You can indeed become the product of your own creation—not the projection viewed from the lenses of others.

You are indeed self-responsible! As my dear friend, Professor William Guillory, puts it in his wonderful book *Realizations:* "Personal empowerment comes through self-awareness."

The Asclepiads, members of an order of physicians in ancient Greece, used humor, drama, magic, and mysticism to teach self-responsibility for thought and action. When properly prepared, a suffering victim would experience a liberating dream and walk away healed in mind and body. A return to old thought patterns, however, would be followed by the onset of the old disease. The magic of the Asclepiads is inherent in our acceptance of self-responsibility. You *are* what you *choose* to be. As Pythagoras said, "Above all else, honor thyself." Anyone who has studied his Golden Verses would conclude that had Pythagoras anticipated the appetite of twentieth-century western culture for reasons, he would have added, "for not to do so is to prevent thine honor of all else."

Good luck, and may you choose all things wisely! Find joy in everything you experience, and all good things will be added. Joy is ultimately the highest expression of unconditional love—and that is who you really are.

For more information regarding subliminal communication, write:

Subliminal Communication
P.O. Box 12419 Las Vegas, Nevada 89112

73

APPENDIX A

COVER SUBLIMINAL

APPENDIX B

PROPOSED 1986 UTAH LEGISLATION

Legislative General Counsel
Approved for Filing: DAT
Date: 12/13/85; 11:44 AM
(Subliminal Communication as Invasion of Privacy)
1986
General Session
H.B. 106   By Frances Hatch Merrill
We oppose surreptitious manipulation for purposes of exploitation.

An act relating to the judicial code; designating subliminal communication without notification as an invasion of privacy; providing remedies; defining terms; and providing a severability clause.

This act affects sections of Utah Code Annotated 1953 as follows:

Enacts:

Chapter 17, Title 78, Utah Code Annotated 1953 Be it enacted by the Legislature of the state of Utah:

Section 1. Chapter 17, Title 78, Utah Code Annotated 1953, is enacted to read:

78-17-1. As used in this chapter, "subliminally embedded communication" means any device or technique that is intentionally used to convey or attempt to convey a message to a person by means of images, writing, or sounds which are not consciously perceivable.

78-17-2. It is an invasion of privacy for any person in this state to convey or cause to be conveyed to any individual any communication which the person knows or should know contains a subliminally embedded communication, unless the person:

(1) makes or causes to be made a notification, in the manner required by Section 78-17-3, of the existence of the subliminally embedded communication; and

(2) provides to the individual, on request, a written description of the content of the subliminally embedded communication.

78-17-3. The notification required by Section 78-17-2 shall:

(1) be reasonably calculated to notify persons to whom the subliminally embedded communication may be transmitted of the existence of the subliminally embedded communication;

(2) include a notification of the availability of a written description of the content of the subliminally embedded communication and of the name and address of the person conveying it or causing it to be conveyed, for use by individuals to whom the communication is conveyed in obtaining the written description;

(3)(a) be made in conspicuously placed and easily legible type, if the communication is intended to be seen; or

(b) be made in a clearly audible manner immediately prior to the communication being made, if the communication is intended to be heard; and

(4) in addition to the requirements of Subsection (3), be made in conspicuously placed and easily legible type on the face of any label or packaging of the medium containing the communication, whether the communication is intended to be seen or heard.

78-17-4. Any individual whose privacy has been invaded as a result of an act described in this chapter, or the state of Utah, may maintain an action to enjoin the continuance of the subliminally embedded communication until the person conveying the communication or causing it to be conveyed makes or causes to be made the notification described in Section 78-17-2 and provides a written description of the content of the subliminally embedded communication to any person requesting it. Actual damages need not be alleged or proved to support the injunction.

78-17-5. In addition to or in lieu of the remedy provided in Section 78-17-3, an individual whose privacy has been invaded as a result of an act described in this chapter may maintain an action against the person who conveyed the communication or caused it to be conveyed for the recovery of three times his actual damages, for punitive damages, and for costs of suit, including reasonable attorney's fees.

Section 2. If any provision of this act, or the application of any provision to any person or circumstance, is held invalid, the remainder of this act is given effect without the invalid provision or application.

Legislative General Counsel
Approved for Filing: DAT
Date: 12/13/85; 11:41 AM
(Subliminal Communication As Unfair Competition)
1986
General Session
H.B. 107   By Frances Hatch Merrill

An act relating to commerce and trade; amending the unfair practices act to include subliminal communication without notification as unfair competition; defining terms; and providing a severability clause.

This act affects sections of Utah Code Annotated 1953 as follows:

Enacts:

13-5-3.1, Utah Code Annotated 1953

Be it enacted by the Legislature of the state of Utah:

Section 1. Section 13-5-3.1, Utah Code Annotated 1953, is enacted to read:

13-5-3.1. (1) As used in this section, "subliminally embedded communication" means any device or technique that is intentionally used to convey or attempt to convey a message to a person by means of images, writing, or sounds which ar not consciously perceived.

(2) It is an unfair method of competition in commerce or trade for any person in this state to convey or cause to be conveyed to the public a communication intended to result in monetary gain which the person knows or should know contains a subliminally embedded communication, or to manufacture, distribute, or sell in this state any printed, audio, or visual medium which the person knows or should know contains a subliminally embedded communication, unless the person:

(a) makes or causes to be made a notification, in the manner required by Subsection (3), of the existence of the subliminally embedded communication; and

(b) provides to any person, on request, a written description of the content of the subliminally embedded communication.

(3) The notification required by Subsection (2)(a) shall:

(a) be reasonably calculated to notify persons to whom the subliminally embedded communication may be transmitted of the existence of the subliminally embedded communication;

(b) include a notification of the availability of a written description of the content of the subliminally embedded communication and of the name and address of the person conveying it or causing it to be conveyed, for use by persons to whom the communication is conveyed in obtaining the written description;

(c)(i) be made in conspicuously placed and easily legible type, if the communication is intended to be seen; or

(ii) be made in a clearly audible manner immediately prior to the communication being made, if the communication is intended to be heard; and

(d) in addition to the requirements of Subsection (2)(c), be made in conspicuously placed and easily legible type on the face of any label or packaging of the medium containing the communication, whether the communication is intended to be seen or heard.

Section 2. If any provision of this act, or the application of any provision to any person or circumstance, is held invalid, the remainder of this act is given effect without the invalid provision or application.

Legislative General Counsel
Approved for Filing: DAT
Date: 12/13/85; 11:30 AM
(Subliminal Communication Cause of Action)
1986
General Session
H.B. 108   By Frances Hatch Merrill

An act relating to the judicial code; creating a civil cause of action for injury or death caused by subliminal communication; defining terms; and providing a severability clause.

This act affects sections of Utah Code Annotated 1953 as follows:

Enacts:

78-11-7.5, Utah Code Annotated 1953

Be it enacted by the Legislature of the state of Utah:

Section 1. Section 78-11-7.5, Utah Code Annotated 1953, is enacted to read:

78-11-7.5. (1) An action for damages resulting from injury or death of a person may be maintained by the person or, as permitted by Sections 78-11-6 and 78-11-7, his parent, guardian, heirs, or personal representative, against a person who knowingly communicated or caused to be communicated a subliminally embedded communication which proximately resulted in the injury or death.

(2) As used in this section, "subliminally embedded communication" means any device or technique that is intentionally used to convey or attempt to convey a message to a person by means of images, writing, or sounds which are not consciously perceived.

Section 2. If any provision of this act, or the application of any provision to any person or circumstance, is held invalid, the remainder of this act is given effect without the invalid provision or application.

TALK-RADIO DISCUSSION HIGHLIGHTS

Taylor: I understand the intent of this legislation is to eliminate willful exploitation of the public via subliminal technology.

Jessop: That's correct, Eldon.

Taylor: The Mind Mint thoroughly supports that. Not to support it is un-American. Virgil, you correct me if I get it wrong, but in reviewing the bills myself, I have some problems because the language is rather ambiguous and by definition perhaps could tie the hands of our behavioral scientists, our self-help community, and for that matter maybe even the conversations a mom might have with her child. This is where you are coming from, is that right?

Hayes: I believe that could possibly be the interpretation—as vague as the interpretation is, and I think that's what we're here to address tonight, Eldon. So I think that it might be appropriate if we were to have a partial reading of the bills so that the public might have more of an idea what the bill actually states.

Jessop: Basically we have three bills. H.B. 106 is primarily discussing the use of subliminal communication as an invasion of privacy. It is our contention that an individual has the right to be subjected to whatever they want to be subjected to as long as they have prior notification that they are going to be subjected to this. That's one of the reasons why we believe that it will be found constitutional is because we are not trying to outlaw all subliminals. What the state would be able to do is regulate, with prior notification, any use of subliminals, whether that is done through a professional hypnotherapist, whether it is done in the recording industry, advertising industry, grocery stores, or whatever. Basically, if you go into a doctor's office, you say, "Doctor, I'm sick; I need some help." The doctor would then perhaps administer a prescription or other things that he felt were reasonable. Usually the patient does not say, "Hey, would you tell me what this particular prescription has to do with the healing process?" And so, usually we just let the doctor do whatever he wants to do.

What we would like is, that if a person is going to be subjected to subliminal messages, that is fine as long as the person is aware that they are going to be subjected to subliminal messages. We are definitely aware that there are positive uses of subliminal messages. For example, to help a person lose weight, stop smoking, perhaps to modify deviant sexual behavior, cut down shoplifting, there are positive uses of subliminals; not all subliminal uses are of a negative nature.

Kirkwood: Yes, I even own one. It is the 23rd Psalm subliminal and I listen to it as I drive around.

Jessop: . . . positive mental attitude, so many things. We have no conflict with Mr. Hayes or with anyone else interested in being able to use subliminals, provided the individual is aware that they are in a contractual basis, that they are actually receiving subliminals, and that they have the opportunity to receive a transcript of these additionally encoded messages.

Kirkwood: So if that [subliminal message] should be in a cassette or record, it should be on the jacket or something like that?

Jessop: At least notification that there is a subliminal message inside and then a place where they can contact the producers of that particular subliminal message.

Taylor: That is the intent of 106 and 107?

Jessop: Yes.

Taylor: Now, how about 108?

82

Kirkwood: Starting with those is there any objection to that from either one of you?

Hayes: Well, I'd like to start out by saying we are not here as the American Council to be in defense of subliminal signals or subliminal advertising or exploitation. However, we are opposed to H.B. 106, as the intent of the author is substantially different than the writing of 106, in my interpretation. The proposal of 106 is incredibly vague, not specific to the areas of actual concern. We believe that this proposal is not only unenforceable but does not even remotely address the specific problem areas. Now, we do agree with the legislative attorney that this bill could possibly deny freedom of speech as well as freedom of press, and possibly as well to think in ways that are most appropriate to the individual without having legislation. We also believe that 106 should be dismissed or rewritten to meet the specific cause of concern as quickly as possible. We also believe that this bill is unconstitutional and we cannot protect the public from reality; however, what we can do is train the public and educate the public to respond to reality. We believe that education, not legislation is the answer. We also believe that H.B. 106 will create far more problems than it would eliminate. We believe that far more input from those who are experts in the field of communication is necessary to assist in rewriting this proposed bill towards the specific purposes and intent. And we are in agreement as to the intent of H.B. 106. However, in our opinion, as written, it is nonspecific, nondirectional and does not even address the specific issues, and we are on record as opposing H.B. 106 for that reason.

Kirkwood: Okay, now . . . so far the intent of the bill is to require notification that there is a subliminal like on a tape or record, radio, and TV. I guess those would be. . . . Of course you couldn't regulate radio and television, could you?

Jessop: Yes, if it created . . . if the advertisements are created within the state and broadcast within the state, yes.

Kirkwood: Is there any problem with that?

Hayes: Well, actually the writing of the bill in itself and the reason we are opposed is because definition in effect covers any and all communication between any and all individuals, i.e., sounds through verbal content and/or nonverbal facial expressions, body positions, style of clothes, hair styles, images, love letters, writing newspapers, books, and will prohibit any of these mediums without making the communicator by law a psychic. So that they may become aware of the subliminally transmitted messages as received by the communicatee.

Kirkwood: Where does that say that in there?

Hayes: In the definition, right? . . . Let me borrow the bill . . . Right there, and I want to read that to you.

Kirkwood: Yes, the specific areas now.

Hayes: That's why we needed to read that . . . The definition as used in this chapter . . . "subliminally embedded communication means any device or technique that is intentionally used to convey or attempt to convey a message to a person by means of images, writings, or sounds which are not consciously perceived." And as we have agreed, as most communicators have agreed, that a vast majority of any and all communication is of a subliminal nature, now this could be something even as simple as a baby crying in the middle of the night at 2:00 a.m. to wake mom up. . . .

Kirkwood: The bill says intentionally though.

Hayes: The *intentionally. Intentionally* means anytime we communicate with an individual.

Kirkwood: Intentionally . . . does it say intentionally to use subliminal . . . ?

Hayes: To convey or attempt to convey a message to a person by means, images, writings, or sounds which are not consciously perceived, and the fact is the vast majority of communication, whether it's me presenting myself to you on the street socially, has subliminal implications and I think that these need to be cleaned up and addressed so that it doesn't restrict any and all communicators to hang out a sign each time they make a statement to someone such as have a nice day, for example, because of the subliminal implications behind that statement. If a person is having a good day, they might have that amplified; if they're having bad day, they might take the opposite approach, the reversal effect, and these things are subconscious functions, subliminal functions.

Kirkwood: Terry, you are the director of the National Institute of Subliminal Research; what does that mean?

Jessop: Basically, what our organization is interested in doing is monitoring the use of possibly sexual or satanical subliminals as they're used in magazines, newspapers, television, motion pictures across the United States. People, members of our organization and those who are not, make it possible for us to receive copies or notification of those particular messages which they feel perhaps are documented sources. Basically, where we are coming from is we feel that this is perhaps an extreme interpretation. As we have met with some very responsible lawyers, we have felt that this is not that case; however, I don't feel like it is such a personal thing that I would feel offended if some of the terminology were changed, but as we have been able to speak with the attorneys and as I have had a chance to go through and look at the legislation, I believe it is very responsible, very reasonable, and that's basically where I am coming from.

Hayes: Well, the legislative attorney himself in his report as to the intent of this, 106, 107, and 108, made the statement that it may be challenged on the basis of the federal First Amendment and state constitutional rights to freedom of speech and press and in this particular situation I believe that it would not only do that but it would restrict that freedom of speech as well as press. So, when the term *responsible attorney* has been made I think that this comes from the legislative attorney and I don't know of anyone more responsible in the state.

Taylor: Mr. Taggert, if I am correct, is quoted in today's newspapers as stating. Virgil, that "juries will decide what is a subliminal message." And, he added, it's a problem of proof, but the law is there to say there is a probable cause of action for, so the entire interpretation if I am understanding this correctly, the entire interpretation of what constitutes a subliminal is something that Taggert is saying a jury would decide.

Hayes: Well, in that particular case, getting back to the subliminal contents. To begin with, as we both know in our particular professions, people can see, hear, and feel what they want to in response to any given stimuli, and we regulate or

85

create a law that's going to overload our already overloaded systems because the law or because the bill may not be specific. I think that to allow the juries to figure it out in this particular case might tie all of us up in court for the rest of our lives.

Taylor: Very possible.

Hayes: And I think that's a great danger here because of that generalization.

Taylor: Representative Merrill has joined us and we are really pleased to have you here this evening. We'll pass this all to you. Thank you very much for coming.

Kirkwood: Representative Frances Merrill.

Merrill: Thank you.

Kirkwood: Now, you're the primary sponsor of this bill, aren't you?

Merrill: Right.

Kirkwood: Okay. There seems to be some questions about the intent of this bill. Is this the broad, encompassing bill that's going to go after things that the bill isn't designed to do or has the Attorney General's office gone over this with you? I assume they have.

Merrill: No, I have not gone to them to get an opinion.

Kirkwood: Okay, then, what are your feelings? Obviously, Virgil Hayes here has been stating that he feels that this bill is what, much too broad? Representative Merrill, what's your feeling on this? You're sponsoring it, so you obviously have some feelings.

Merrill: Okay, let me tell you where I'm coming from on this bill. I was approached to see if I would be interested in sponsoring this type of legislation and after looking into it I came to the conclusion that it's a subject that needs to be heard, and I'm willing to sponsor it and introduce it up there. Terry Jessop is going to be the spokesman. He is the one that's going to defend it up there. When they ask questions, he's the one that will answer them if they have constitutional questions. The legislative attorneys will be there to answer those and that's the perspective that I am coming from. I think it's a subject that needs to be heard.

Kirkwood: Okay, so you're just a general sponsor rather than specific.

Merrill: That's right.

Kirkwood: Okay, so I guess you need to be here and discuss from your point of view, but coming back to Terry Jessop, you're the primary spokesman.

Merrill: That's right.

Kirkwood: Okay, then Terry, Virgil's comments, let's get some reaction to them.

Jessop: Yes. As we have sat down, whenever one of these bills has been written the attorneys will always put anything that is germane when it has to do with the Constitution. . . . I cannot speak for Mr. Taggert, but as he has spoken with me in the past, he said, "If this legislation is challenged, it would be challenged on the free speech issue, etc." The reason why he feels that it probably would be found constitutional is that we are not prohibiting the use of subliminals. The major emphasis is that an individual has a right to prior notification and that's the basic image that is being presented on a professional basis. We see no reason why a responsible, ethical person, whether it's for commercial use or any other use, would be opposed to giving prior notification, at least that [consumers] are going to be subjected to subliminals.

Hayes: We are in agreement with the intent of the bill, and as I stated to begin with, we are not here to defend subliminals; however, the definition states something entirely different. If you even look at the dictionary definitions of the words that are sued in that definition, being so incredibly broad they re not directed towards any specific purpose. But yet, it could be interpreted through any millions of interpretations and that's where the greatest danger lies in this proposal; not in the intent, but in the proposal itself in the writing of the bill.

Taylor: Now, if I may interject here. Representative Merrill and Terry, I had the opportunity to speak I believe with the co-sponsor, Representative Lloyd Selleniet, and if I understood him correctly, your position on the bill was, it's the intent that is, the object of it: if there were an entanglement, if there were an ambiguity, if there were a problem—and I think I heard you

87

say this earlier, Terry—with a word or with the terminology (if it were too broad, too all-encompassing), you are sensible and you are flexible about it; you would change that or rework it. I'm curious; would that be in the committee or would that be on the floor of the House?

Merrill: Everything is going to be heard in committee tomorrow. All the opposition to it will come in and speak; we will do our little pitch during the committee meeting and I would welcome anybody that is interested in it to come up there and testify whether they're for it or against it. My feeling is it needs to be heard and we would hope that people that are interested in it would come up there. We don't want to pass some law up there that is not going to be good for the people. So, I would say tomorrow is the big day. It may not get out of committee; nobody knows that. We have to wait till tomorrow to see what happens. But we are going to present it and I think if they hear the pros and cons of it, they will make the decision that's right for the people, the state of Utah.

Hayes: Well, according to and going back to what I was saying before, all communication basically contains subliminal elements. Let's say that there proportionately would be absolutely no communication without subliminal elements. I think that you need to write the bill so that it would be appropriately directed towards the specific application such as the 1 percent that are unethical that you had talked about today in the paper. If the 99 percent is being subjected to this bill when in essence it's only 1 percent that is creating the problem, I think that that might be the same situation as using atom bombs to take care of the situation when hand grenades would do.

Jessop: Now, once again, you're still misquoting from the position that was given out of the newspaper. I was talking about advertising agencies, not about subliminal messages per se; basically we feel, I personally feel, that there is a multi-billion-dollar industry out there. Somebody is paying for these subliminals to be produced and it's an extremely expensive type of creation of subliminals. These are being created in television advertisements, motion pictures, etc. Somebody is footing the bill and so I don't believe that by any means that it's only 1 percent of negative subliminals which are encroaching upon our society. If that were the case, perhaps I would not feel so strongly about petitioning very responsible legislators like Representatives Merrill and Selleniet to introduce this legislation. If I could just continue on with this thought. One of the other things that I felt strongly about is, recently there has been a great amount of notoriety having to do with mass-murder slayers, the night stalker in California and many others across the United States, which have been involved in not only mass murders of women but of children, etc. As many people are aware, or perhaps as the populace out there may not be aware, in the background of some music and other programs, there are very strong antisocial messages which maybe say smoke pot, take drugs, commit sexual advances on another person as well as direct commands to kill children, etc. I believe very strongly that an individual that can prove in a court of law that, for example, say the survivors of the family of the child that has been killed, can prove that there has been significant evidence that that murderer was influenced substantially enough, should be able to sue the estate of that particular murderer. That's one of the reasons (and that's not the only reason) why we're not going after, for example, the specific recording industry. That is just one example. The technology is very high tech and it's not limited only to the recording industry and that's why, one of the reasons why I feel uncomfortable in trying to create a law only for the recording industry, only for the television industry, etc., but we had discussed this with the attorneys prior to initiating the legislation.

Hayes: I wonder if you are even aware of the tremendous implications behind what you are actually saying, because, as you are aware, there are many more positive uses than negative ones for subliminal signals. Let's say, to be more specific, a section would require a disclaimer any time that a communication was made of the existence of a subliminally embedded communication, i.e., all communication by anyone who spoke, projected an image, facial expressions, type of clothes, etc., wrote a letter, read a newspaper, sat in church or school. Isn't prayer subliminally embedded communication as well as learning in school? Are these people to be required, if this proposed bill is not defeated now, to provide notice of intent, a written description of possible interpretation on the part of the receiver of the possible responses they might have? Basically, that's the interpretation literally in this bill.

Jessop: No, I think that that's a very radical interpretation which is not reasonably projected at all.

Taylor: Back in the fifties we became aware of subliminal technology primarily through the notoriety that was involved when a New Jersey theater flashed "drink Coca-Cola," "eat popcorn," some such thing on Kim Novak's face during a Kim Novak movie. Now, I know that I've talked to hundreds of people that believe there is legislation in place that protects the consumer against covert manipulation via the modality of subliminal techniques, but it's my understanding that that legislation has always broken down.

Jessop: That's correct, Eldon. Actually, many laws have been introduced all over the United States. As I was working with the former attorney general of the state of Utah, we were not able to find any laws which had actually been enacted anywhere in the United States. However, during the last year several bills are in various forms at least in California, New York, New Jersey, and Pennsylvania. There are some codes saying we would recommend that you don't do this or we would recommend you don't do that, but as far as actually having anyone ever go to jail, pay a fine, or whatever, I am not aware of any actual legislation which has been passed in the United States.

Merrill: The attorneys who drafted the bill think it is constitutional. I personally am concerned about the privacy of my own mind. And I don't want to have that invaded. That's why I am interested in these bills. So I'm interested to see what the discussion is tomorrow, and nobody can give the answer. If it ever goes to court on any of these issues, there is a jury probably that will decide the outcome of it. I can't predict that and neither can anybody else.

Kirkwood: I think Representative Merrill is representing a lot of us who are very concerned. I was just complaining to my wife about a week ago about a television commercial; the light

90

comes off of a young body in a way that she looks very ordinary but the light hits her and it's a subliminal message and it's very sexual. And this is what's going on on television and I think, how do you fight that?

Hayes: Well, I think that it might be far more appropriate rather than attempting to legislate morality for an example . . .

Kirkwood: No, no, no, no.

Hayes: . . . that what we might want to attempt to do is educate the individual how to utilize the conscious functioning so that they can reject those ideas at a time when it's appropriate for them because isn't the H.B. 106, 107, and 108 in and of itself an invasion of privacy of those who do choose to indulge in that type of programming?

Kirkwood: All legislation is morality.

Taylor: I don't think it's an invasion of privacy, as a matter of fact. I think what they're asking for is just labeling and I'm all for that.

Jessop: Prior notification is what we're after.

Taylor: If you want to buy a record that is by a heavy-metal group that has "smoke marijuana," "kill a baby" on it, okay. I guess consenting adults, I don't know. Maybe that's even being treated. What you mentioned on television, Jim, that's an issue I think is called supraliminal. Through association very often we will see a politician with a flag behind him, you're going to be aware of that flag. Well, that's subliminal in a sense, but it's been defined, as I understand it, as supraliminal because the conscious mind has the capability of recognizing the purpose of that association. But when you mention what you see on television, Terry has, as I understand it, an audio-video presentation that will be shown to the legislative committee tomorrow, as well as anyone and everyone that is there. I've seen some of the slides and of course we've talked about some of Professor Key's work *Clam Plate Orgy* and *Subliminal Seduction,* and I've seen some of the material on slides straight out of those books. It's a very real menace to our society. Are we really opposed to that?

AMENDMENTS TO THE PROPOSED 1986 UTAH LEGISLATION

House
Committee Amendments
January 29, 1986

Representative Merrill proposes the following amendments to H.B. 106, Subliminal Communication As Invasion of Privacy.

Page 1, Lines 19-22: Delete Section 78-17-1 in its entirety and insert the following in its place:

78-17-1. "Subliminally embedded communication" means any visual image, writing, or sound which is intentionally placed in any printing, audio, or visual medium in order to draw attention to the subject of the medium without the visual image, writing, or sound being consciously perceived, or in order to directly convey or attempt to convey a message which is not consciously perceived. It does not include images or impressions which are conveyed by implication or by visual images or a series of visual images which are consciously perceived.

Utah H.B. 106

Subject: Subliminal Communication as Invasion of Privacy

Suggested amendments:

Add as Section 78-17-6 (page 3 of the Bill):

78-17-6. The provisions of this chapter shall not apply to any entity whose only participation in the conveyance of such messages is as a provider of facilities or services for the transmission of communications to the public.

THURSTONE MEASUREMENT TABLE

The Thurstone Temperament Scale measures seven different areas of the subject's personality:

Activity

Vigorousness

Impulsiveness

Dominance

Stability

Sociability

Reflectivity

The figures on the following pages show pretest and posttest measurements taken in connection with the study of the effects of subliminal communication on inmates at the Utah State Prison.

Adult Profile

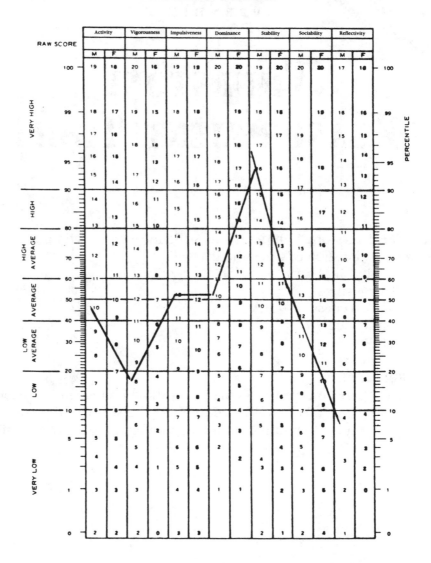

Figure 1. Pretest measurement.

Adult Profile

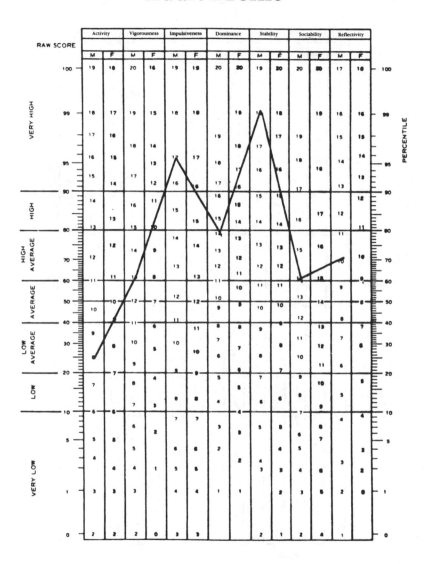

Figure 2. Posttest measurement.

95

Adult Profile

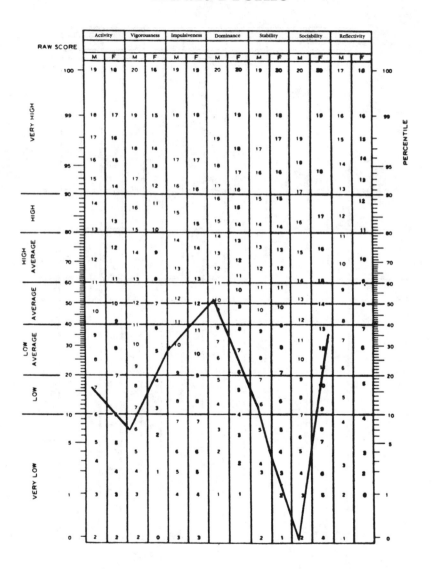

Figure 3. Pretest measurement.

Adult Profile

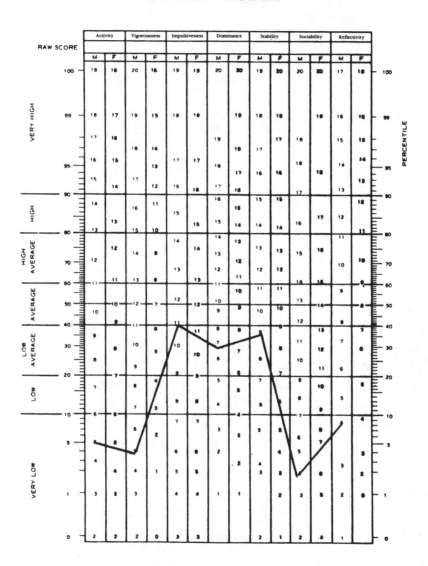

Figure 4. Posttest measurement.

97

ABSTRACT OF FINDINGS

by *CHARLES F. McCLUSKER*

Thirty-eight male residents (average age, twenty-three) from the Unit at the Utah State Prison completed the Thurstone Temperament Schedule in a voluntary participatory study. Following administration, subjects were randomly placed in one of three groups (experimental, fourteen; placebo, thirteen; and control, eleven). The experimental group received and played a subliminal tape for twenty days. The placebo group received and played a similar sounding tape without an embedded subliminal message, while the control group had no tape exposure. At the end of twenty days a second Thurstone Temperament Schedule was administered. In the experimental group five subjects remained who had completed the procedure, three in the placebo, and eight in the control. Others were lost due to discharges or unwillingness to participate.

In a comparison of the experimental and control groups, the following results were obtained. The Dominance scale scores decreased while the Reflective and Stability scale scores increased in the Experimental group (desired effects). The Dominance scale scores increased while the Reflective scale scores decreased in the Control group. These are interesting results across groups. In the experimental group these results would be predicted by focus of the embedded subliminal messages. In the placebo group the opposite effect obtained may be explained by the fact that they (the subjects) listened to a tape without a message and felt no change. They obtained no reinforcement to continue, and possibly experienced some frustration.

It is stressed that this pilot study had limitations, especially in time of implementation and sample size.

It is not the intention of the experimenters to generalize beyond the obtained results. It must be stressed, however, that to evaluate an incarcerated population was a unique opportunity; to our knowledge this was the first time subliminal technology has been evaluated with this population. The results indicated change and strongly suggest the need for further research with benefit to these individuals and society in general, as this technology is better understood and applied in a wide variety of applications and settings.

Experimental			Control		
Predifferences to postdifferences			Predifferences to postdifferences		
Scale Movement	Variable	Rate of Change	Scale Movement	Variable	Rate of Change
↑	Stability	+ 3.4	↑	Stability	+ .8
↑	Reflectivity	+ 2.6	↓	Reflectivity	−1.0
↓	Dominance	−2.7	↑	Dominance	+ 1.4

Figure 5. Comparisons between the experimental group and the control group.

99

RECOMMENDED READINGS

Adams, V. May 1982. "Mommy and I are one": Beaming messages to inner space. *Psychology Today,* 16 (9), 24.

Adamson, R.; Henke, P.; and O'Donovan, D. 1969. Avoidance conditioning following preadaptation to weak shock. *Psychonomic Science,* 14 (3), 119–21.

Advertising Age. 28 Feb. 1985, p. 6. Ads against wall in video background.

Advertising Age. 13 Aug. 1984, p. 6. Spirits industry beams over BATF review.

Advertising Age. 14 June 1982, p. 63. *New Woman* magazine has developed what it calls "subliminal synergism," a technique whereby the dominant color or colors of a four-color ad page are picked up on the page opposite as a color-coded tint block behind a headline.

Advertising Age. 5 Jan. 1981, p. 36. Inappropriate modifiers can seriously water down an ad message, warns Social Research, Inc. Chicago: BB Gardner.

American Metal Market. 16 Aug. 1984, p. 14. Shoplifting reduced 80 percent by subliminal technology.

Andersson, A. L.; Fries, I.; and Smith, G. J. 1970. Change in afterimage and spiral aftereffect serials due to anxiety caused by subliminal threat. *Scandinavian Journal of Psychology,* 11 (1), 7–17.

Antell, M. J. Feb. 1970. The effect of priming and the subliminal presentation of sexual and aggressive stimuli on tests of creativity. *Dissertation Abstracts International,* 30 (8–B), 3859–60.

Antell, J. J., and Goldberger, L. 1978. The effects of subliminally presented sexual and aggressive stimuli on literary creativity. *Psychological Research Bulletin,* Lund Univ., 19 (7), 20.

Ariam, S., and Siller, J. Oct. 1982. Effects of subliminal oneness stimuli in Hebrew on academic performance of Israeli high school students: Further evidence on the adaptation-enhancing effects of symbiotic fantasies in another culture using another language. *Journal of Abnormal Psychology,* 91 (5).

Arzumanov, IuL. Sept.-Oct. 1974. Elaboration of temporary connections in man using unrecognized visual stimuli. *Zh Vyssh Nerv Deiat,* 24 (5), 917–23.

Augenbraun, H. R. June 1983. The effect of subliminal activation of unconscious fantasies in the treatment of juvenile-onset and adult-onset obesity. *Dissertation Abstracts International,* 43 (12–B), 4134.

Babighian, G. July-Aug. 1969. Behavior and clinical importance of various subliminal tests in Menier's disease. *Minerva Otorinolaringo* (Italy), 19 (4), 215–22.

Bagby, P. K. June 1985. The effect of symbiotic and oedipal subliminal stimuli on field independence and competitive tasks. *Dissertation Abstracts International,* 45 (12–B, Pt 1), 3927.

Baker, L. E. 1937. The influence of subliminal stimuli upon verbal behavior. *Journal of Experimental Psychology,* 20.

Balota, D. A. June 1982. Automatic and attention activation in semantic and episodic memory: Implications for the utility of conscious awareness. *Dissertation Abstracts International,* 42 (12–B, Pt 1), 4952.

Bancroft, W. J. 1976. Suggestology and suggestopedia: The theory of the Lozanov method.

Banreti-Fuchs, K. M. 1967. Perception without awareness. *Acta Psychologia* (Amsterdam, Netherlands), 26 (2), 148–60.

Barber, P. J., and Rushton, J. F. Aug. 1975. Experimenter bias and subliminal perception. *British Journal of Psychology,* 66 (3), 357–72.

Barchas, P. R., and Perlaki, K. M. June 1986. Processing of preconsciously acquired information measured by hemispheric asymmetry and selection accuracy. *Behav Neurosci,* 100 (3), 343–49.

102

Barenklau, K. E. Dec. 1981. Using subliminals in technical training. *Training,* 18 (1), 50–51.

Bargh, J. A.; Bond, R. N.; Lombardi, W. J.; and Tota, M. E. May 1986. The additive nature of chronic and temporary sources of construct accessibility. *Journal of Personality and Social Psychology,* 50 (5), 869–78.

Barkoczi, I.; Sera, L.; and Komlosi, A. Mar. 1983. Relationships between functional asymmetry of the hemispheres, subliminal perception, and some defense mechanisms in various experimental settings. *Psychologia: An International Journal of Psychology in the Orient,* 26 (1), 1–20.

Battersby, W. S., and Defabaugh, G. L. July 1969. Neural limitations of visual excitability: After-effects of subliminal stimulation. *Vision Research* (England), 9 (7), 757–68.

Bauer, W. Feb. 1986. The effects of conditional and unconditional subliminal symbiotic stimuli on intrinsic motivation. *Dissertation Abstracts International,* 46 (8–B), 2794–95.

Becker, H. C.; Chamberlain S.; Burt, S.; Heisse, J.; and Marino, D. Poster session reported to the American Society of Clinical Hypnosis, 25th Annual Scientific Meeting.

Becker, H. C., and Charbonnet, K. D. 28 Mar. 1980. Applications of subliminal video and audio stimuli in therapeutic, educational, industrial, and commercial settings. Eighth Annual Northeast Bioengineering Conference, Massachusetts Institute of Technology, Cambridge.

Becker, H. C., and McDonagh, E. W. Nov. 1979. Subliminal communication (subliminal psychodynamic activation) in rehabilitative and preventive medicine. *Proceedings of the Ninth Annual Conference of the Society for Computer Medicine.* Atlanta.

Becker, H. C., and Glauzer, N. H. 10–12 Apr. 1978. Subliminal communication: Advances in audiovisual engineering applications for behavior therapy and education. *Proceedings of the 1978 Institute of Electrical and Electronics Engineering Region 3 Conference.*

Becker, H. C.; Jewell, J. F.; and Alito, P. 13–17 Mar. 1977. Video and audio signal monitors/processors for subliminal communication in weight control. *Proceedings of the 112th Annual Meeting of the Association for the Advancement of Medical Instrumentation* (AAMI). San Francisco.

Becker, H. C., and Elder, S. T. 5–11 Sept. 1966. Can subliminal perception be useful to the psychiatrist? *Excerpta Medica* (International Congress Series No. 117). Abstract of paper presented to the IV World Congress of Psychiatry, Madrid.

Becker, H. C.; Corrigan, R. E.; Elder, S. T.; Tallant, J. D.; and Goldstein, M. 22–27 Aug. 1965. Subliminal communication: biological engineering considerations. In *Digest of the 6th International Conference on Medical Electronics and Biological Engineering,* pp. 452–53. Tokyo.

Beisgen, R. T., Jr.; and Gibby, R. G., Jr. 1969. Virginia Commonwealth Univ. Autonomic and verbal discrimination of a subliminally learned task. *Perceptual and Motor Skills,* 29 (2), 503–7.

Beloff, J. May 1973. The subliminal and the extrasensory. *Parapsychology Review,* 4 (3), 23–27.

Ben-Hur, A. Nov. 1970. The relationship of systematic desensitization and the activation of symbiotic merging fantasy to speech anxiety reduction among college students. *Dissertation Abstracts International,* 40 (5– B), 2351–52.

Bernstein, B. R. Feb. 1986. The effects of subliminal symbiotic and oedipal stimuli on weight loss in obese women. *Dissertation Abstracts International,* 46 (8–B), 2795.

Berry, D. M. May 1985. Effects of educative/support groups and subliminal psychodynamic activation on bulimia in college women. *Dissertation Abstracts International,* 45 (11–B), 3612.

Bevin, W. Feb. 1964. Subliminal stimulation: A pervasive problem for psychology. *Psychological Bulletin,* 61 (2), 84–92.

Block, M. P., and Vanden Bergh, B. G. 1985. Michigan State Univ. Can you sell subliminal messages to consumers? *Journal of Advertising,* 14 (3), 59–62.

Bohm, D., and Peat, D. 1987. *Science, Order and Creativity.* New York: Bantam.

Borgeat, F. Dec. 1983. Psychophysiological effects of two different relaxation procedures: Progressive relaxation and subliminal relaxation. *Psychiatric Journal of the University of Ottawa,* 8 (4), 181–85.

Borgeat, F., and Chaloult, L. Mar. 1985. A relaxation experiment using radio broadcasts. *Canada's Mental Health,* 33 (1), 11–13.

Borgeat, F.; Elie, R.; Chaloult, L.; and Chabot, R. Feb. 1985. Psychophysiological responses to masked auditory stimuli. *Canadian Journal of Psychiatry,* 30 (1), 22–27.

Borgeat, F., and Pannetier, M. F. 1982. Value of cumulative electrodermal responses in subliminal auditory perception: A preliminary study. *Encephale,* 8 (4), 487–99.

Borgeat, F.; Chabot, R.; and Chaloult, L. June 1981. Subliminal perception and level of activation. *Canadian Journal of Psychiatry,* 26 (4), 255–59.

Bouchard, S. J. Dec. 1984. Effects of a self-administered subliminal relaxation treatment on anxiety. *Dissertation Abstracts International,* 45 (6–B), 1906.

Bower, B. Fall 1986. Newsletter article, Is it all in the mind? Institute of Noetic Sciences.

Bower, B. 8 Mar. 1978. Subliminal messages: Changes for the better? *Science News,* 129 (3), 156.

Brandeis, D., and Lehmann, D. 1986. Event-related potentials of the brain and cognitive processes: Approaches and applications. *Neuropsychologia,* 24 (1), 151–68.

Brennan, S. M. Dec. 1984. The effect of subliminal separation-individuation schemas on moral reasoning and mood in depressed and nondepressed women. *Dissertation Abstracts International,* 45 (6–B), 1907.

Bromfield, R. N. May 1986. Subliminal psychodynamic activation: Demonstration, oedipal factors and personality correlates. *Dissertation Abstracts International,* 46 (11–B), 4005.

Bronstein, A. A. Mar. 1983. An experimental study of internalization fantasies in schizophrenic men. *Psychotherapy: Theory, Research and Practice,* 20 (4), 408–16.

Brosgole, L., and Contino, A. F. June 1973. Intrusion of subthreshold learning upon later performance. *Psychological Reports,* 32 (3), 795–99.

Brush, J. Oct. 1982. Subliminal stimulation in asthma: Imaginal, associative, and physiological effects. *Dissertation Abstracts International,* 43 (4–B), 1294–95.

Bryant-Tuckett, R. M. June 1981. The effects of subliminal merging stimuli on the academic performance of emotionally handicapped students. *Dissertation Abstracts International,* 41 (12–B), 4654.

Bryant-Tuckett, R., and Silverman, L. H. July 1984. Effects of the subliminal stimulation of symbiotic fantasies on the academic performance of emotionally handicapped students. *Journal of Counseling Psychology,* 31 (3), 295–305.

105

Budzynski, T. 1977. Tuning in on the twilight zone. *Psychology Today*, 11 (3), 38–44.

Building Supply and Home Centers (formerly *Building Supply News*). Apr. 1987, pp. 88–94. Crooked employees.

Burkham, P. Apr. 1982. The effect of subliminal presentation of two gratifying fantasies on female depressives. *Dissertation Abstracts International*, 42 (10–B), 4183.

Business Week Industrial Edition. 19 May 1986, pp. 126–28. Reeling and dealing: Video meet Wall Street.

Carroll, R. T. July 1980. Neurophysiological and psychological mediators of response to subliminal perception: The influence of hemisphericity and defensive style on susceptibility to subliminally presented conflict-laden stimuli. *Dissertation Abstracts International*, 41 (1–B), 342–43.

Carter, R. Jan.-Feb. 1986. Whispering soft nothings to the shop thief: How "reinforcement messaging" works. *Retail and Distribution Management* (UK), 14 (1), 36, 39.

Chain Store Age Executive Edition. July 1986, pp. 85, 88. Subliminal messages: Subtle crime stoppers.

Chaloult, L.; Borgeat, F.; and Chabot, R. Dec. 1980. Subliminal perception. 1. Its nature and the controversy engendered. *Union Med Can*, 109 (12), 694–700.

Charman, D. K. 1979. An examination of relationships between subliminal perception, visual information processing, levels of processing, and hemispheric asymmetries. *Perceptual and Motor Skills*, 49 (2), 451–55.

Cheesman, J., and Merikle, P. M. Oct. 1984. Priming with and without awareness. *Perception and Psychophysics*, 36 (4), 387–95.

Citrin, M. D. May 1980. The effects of subliminal oedipal stimulation on competitive performance in college males and females. *Dissertation Abstracts International*, 40 (11–B), 5399–5400.

Claire, J. B. 1981. A holographic model of a psychosomatic pattern: Freud's specimen dream reinterpreted. *Psychotherapy and Psychosomatics*, 36 (2), 132–42.

Cohen, R. O. Nov. 1977. The effects of four subliminally introduced merging stimuli on the psychopathology of schizophrenic women. *Dissertation Abstracts International*, 38 (5–B), 2356–57.

Computer Decisions. 29 Jan. 1985, p. 26. Suggestive software.

Cook, H. Fall 1985. Effects of subliminal symbiotic gratification and the magic of believing on achievement. *Psychoanalytic Psychology,* 2 (4), 365–71.

Cooper, C., and Kline, P. Feb. 1986. An evaluation of the Defense Mechanism Test. *British Journal of Psychology,* 77 (1), 10–32.

Crawford, M. A. Aug. 1985. Subliminal messaging—50s technology enjoys a rebirth. *Security Management,* 29 (8), 54–56.

Cuperfain, R., and Clarke, T. K. 1985. A new perspective of subliminal perception. *Journal of Advertising,* 14 (1), 36–41.

Czyzewksa-Pacewicz, M. 1984. The priming phenomenon in semantic memory evoked by subthreshold stimuli. *Przeglad Psychologiczny,* 27 (3), 617–29.

Dauber, R. B. Feb. 1984. Subliminal psychodynamic activation in depression: On the role of autonomy issues in depressed college women. *Journal of Abnormal Psychology,* 93 (1), 9–18.

Dean, D., and Nash, C. B. 1967. Coincident plethysmograph results under controlled conditions. *Journal of the Society of Psychical Research,* 44 (731), 1–14.

DeChenne, J. A. Oct. 1976. An experimental study to determine if a task involving psychomotor and problem solving skills can be taught subliminally. *Dissertation Abstracts International,* 37 (4–A), 1947.

DeHaan, H. J. A speech-rate intelligibility/comprehensibility threshold for speeded and time-compressed connected speech. U.S. Army Research Institute for the Behavioral and Social Sciences, 1978 (June) TB 297.

de Martino, C. R. 1969. The effects of subliminal stimulation as a function of stimulus content, drive arcusal and priming, and defense against drive. *Dissertation Abstracts International,* 29 (12–B), 4843.

Dixon, N. 1981. *Preconscious Processing.* New York: Wiley.

Dixon, N. F. 1983. Data from different areas of research are reviewed to develop a flow model to explain how physiological events in the brain give rise to representations in the mind. *Archiv für Psychologie,* 135 (1), 55–66.

Dixon, N. F. 1981. The conscious/unconscious interface: Contributions to an understanding. *Psychological Research Bulletin,* Lund Univ., 21 (5), 15.

Dixon, N. F. May-June 1979. Subliminal perception and parapsychology: Points of contact. *Parapsychology Review,* 10 (3), 1–6.

Dixon, N. F. 1971. *Subliminal Perception: The Nature of a Controversy*. London: McGraw-Hill.

Dixon, N. F. 1968. "Perception without awareness": A reply to K. M. Bainrelti-Fuchs. *Acta Psychologica* (Amsterdam, Netherlands), 28 (2), 171–80.

Dixon, N. F.; Henley, S. H.; and Weir, C. G. Spring 1984. Extraction of information from continuously masked successive stimuli: An exploratory study. *Current Psychological Research and Reviews*, 3 (1), 38–44.

Doerries, L. E., and Harcum, E. R. Aug. 1967. Long-term traces of tachistoscopic word perception. *Perceptual and Motor Skills* (U.S.) 25 (1), 25–33.

Dunham, W. R. 1984. *The Science of Vital Force*. Boston: Damrell and Upham.

Efran, J. S., and Marcia, J. E. 1967. Treatment of fears by expectancy manipulation: An exploratory investigation. *Proceedings of the 75th Annual Convention of the American Psychological Association*, 2, 239–40.

Emmelkamp, P. M., and Straatman, H. 1976. A psychoanalytic reinterpretation of the effectiveness of systematic desensitization: Fact or fiction? *Behaviour Research and Therapy*, 14 (3), 245–49.

Emrich, H., and Heinemann, L. G. 1966. EEG with subliminal perception of emotionally significant words. *Psychologische Forschung*, 29 (4), 285–96.

Erdelyi, M. H. Nov. 1972. Role of fantasy in the Poetzl (emergency) phenomenon. *Journal of Personality and Social Psychology*, 24 (2), 186–90.

Eroelyi, M. H. 1974. A new look at the new look: Perceptual defense and vigilance. *Psychological Review*, 81, 1–25.

Faenza, V. July-Oct. 1966. Conditions of equivocity of the response in relation to the problem of "subliminal perception." *Arch Psicol Neurol Psichiatr* (Italy), 27 (4), 443–55.

Farre, M. Nov.-Dec. 1965. Degree of discernability of the stimulus and perceptive behavior. *Arch Psicol Neurol Psichiatr* (Italy), 26 (6), 566–76.

Feldman, J. B. May 1979. The utilization of the subliminal psychodynamic activation method in the further examination of conscious and unconscious measures of death anxiety. *Dissertation Abstracts International*, 39 (11–B), 5547–48.

Ferguson, M. 1986. *Brain/Mind Bulletin*. Perspective, 11 (9).

Ferguson, M. 1985. *Brain/Mind Bulletin*. Perspective, 7 (4).

Field, G. A. 1974. The unconscious organization. *Psychoanalytic Review*, 61 (3), 333–54.

Fisher, C. 1956. Dreams, images, and perception: A study of unconscious-preconscious relationships. *Journal of the American Psychoanalytic Association*, 4–48.

Fisher, C. B.; Glenwick, D. S.; and Blumenthal, R. S. Aug. 1986. Subliminal oedipal stimuli and competitive performance: An investigation of between-groups effects and mediating subject variables. *Journal of Abnormal Psychology*, 95 (3), 292–24.

Fisher, S. May 1976. Conditions affecting boundary response to messages out of awareness. *Journal of Nervous and Mental Disease*, 162 (5), 313–22.

Fisher, S. Aug. 1975. State Univ. New York. Effects of messages reported to be out of awareness upon the body boundary. *Journal of Nervous and Mental Disease*, 161 (2), 90–99.

Fiss, H. Dec. 1966. The effects of experimentally induced changes in alertness on response to subliminal stimulation. *Journal of Personality and Social Psychology* (U. S.), 34 (4), 577–95.

Florek, W. G. Nov. 1985. An investigation of the effects of stimulating symbiotic fantasies in primipara females. *Dissertation Abstracts International*, 46 (5–B), 1720.

Folio: The Magazine for Magazine Management, Sept. 1982, pp. 32, 34. 'Subliminal synergism'—harmonized color schemes between an ad and facing editorial copy—attracts advertisers to *New Woman* magazine.

Foodman, A. 1976. Hemispheric asymmetrical brain wave indicators of unconscious mental processes. *Journal of Operational Psychiatry*, 7 (1), 3–15.

Foster, R. P. Apr. 1982. The effects of subliminal tachistoscopic presentation of drive-related stimuli on the cognitive functioning of paranoid and nonparanoid schizophrenics. *Dissertation Abstracts International*, 42 (10–B), 4190–91.

Fox, Muriel 1966. Differential effects of subliminal and supraliminal stimulation. *Dissertation Abstracts International*, 27 (4B), 1289–90.

Frauman, D. C.; Lynn, S. J.; Hardaway, R.; and Molteni, A. Nov. 1984. Effect of subliminal symbiotic activation on hypnotic rapport and susceptibility. *Journal of Abnormal Psychology,* 93 (4), 481–483.

Fribourg, A. June 1981. The effect of fantasies of merging with a good-mother figure on schizophrenic pathology. *Journal of Nervous and Mental Disease,* 169 (6), 337–47.

Fribourg, A. Sept. 1979. The effect of fantasies of merging with a good-mother figure on schizophrenic pathology. *Dissertation Abstracts International,* 40 (3–B), 1363.

Friedman, S. 1976. Perceptual registration of the analyst outside of awareness. *Psychoanalytic Quarterly,* 45 (1), 128–30.

Froufe, T. M., and Sierra, D.B. June 1985. Perception without awareness. *Boletin de Psicologia* (Spain), 7, 7–50.

Fulford, P. F. Oct. 1980. The effect of subliminal merging stimuli on test anxiety. *Dissertation Abstracts International,* 41 (4–B), 1503.

Gade, P. A., and Gertman, David. "Listening to compressed speech: The effects of instructions, experience and preference." *U.S. Army Research Institute for the Behavioral and Social Science,* Aug. 1979, TP 369.

Gadlin, W., and Fiss, H. 1967. Odor as a facilitator of the effects of subliminal stimulation. *Journal of Personality and Social Psychology,* 7 (1, Pt. 1), 95–100.

Ganovski, L. 1977. The role of peripheral perceptions in solving mental tasks. *Activitas Nervosa Superior,* 19 (4), 280–81.

Geisler, C. J. Oct. 1986. The use of subliminal psychodynamic activation in the study of repression. *Journal of Personality and Social Psychology* (U. S.), 51 (4), 844–45.

Geisler, C. J. May 1983. A new experimental method for the study of the psychoanalytic concept of repression. *Dissertation Abstracts International,* 43 (11–B), 3757.

Giddan, N. S. Mar. 1967. Recovery through images of briefly flashed stimuli. *Journal Personal Social Psychology* (U.S.), 35 (1), 1–19.

Glaser, M., and Chi, J. 5 Nov. 1984. More competition, slower growth ahead for drug chains/employee theft an "epidemic": Loss prevention chief. *Drug Topics,* 128 (21), 84–85.

Glennon, S. June 1984. The effects of functional brain asymmetry and hemisphericity on the subliminal activation of residual oedipal conflicts. *Dissertation Abstracts International,* 44 (12–B), 3931–32.

Glover, E. D. Mar. 1978. The influence of subliminal perception on smoking behavior. *Dissertation Abstracts International,* 38 (9–A), 5265.

Golland, J. H. 1967. The effects of experimental drive arousal on response to subliminal stimulation. *Dissertation Abstracts International,* 27 (11–B), 4123.

Gordon, C. M., and Spence, D. D. 1966. The facilitating effects of food set and food deprivation on responses to a subliminal food stimulus. *Journal of Personality,* 34Z (3), 406–15.

Gordon, W. K. May 1983. Combination of cognitive group therapy and subliminal stimulation in treatment of test-anxious college males. *Dissertation Abstracts International,* 43 (11–B), 3731.

Grant, R. H. Aug. 1980. The effects of subliminally projected visual stimuli on skill development, selected attention, and participation in racquetball by college students. *Dissertation Abstracts International,* 41 (2–A), 585.

Greenberg, R. P., and Fisher, S. Dec. 1980. Freud's penis–baby equation: Exploratory tests of a controversial theory. *British Journal of Medical Psychology,* 53 (4), 33–42.

Groeger, J. A. Feb. 1986. Predominant and nonpredominant analysis: Effects of level of presentation. *British Journal of Psychology,* 77 (1), 109–16.

Groeger, J. A. Aug. 1984. Evidence of unconscious semantic processing from a forced-error situation. *British Journal of Psychology,* 75 (3), 305–14.

Guillory, W. 1988. Unpublished. Innovations Consulting, Salt Lake City, Utah.

Guthrie, G., and Wiener, M. June 1966. Subliminal perception or perception of partial cue with pictorial stimuli. *Journal Personal Social Psychology* (U.S.), 3 (6), 619–22.

Guttman, G., and Ganglberger, J. 1967. Conditioned verbal reactions triggered by subliminal thalmic stimulation. *Zeitschrift Für Experimentelle und Angewandte Psychologie,* 14 (3), 542–44.

Haberstroh, J. 17 Sept. 1984. Can't ignore subliminal ad changes. *Advertising Age,* 55 (61), 3, 442, 44.

Halpern, S. 1985. *Sound Health.* San Francisco: Harper and Row.

Hardy, G. R., and Legge, D. 1968. Cross-model induction of changes in sensory thresholds. *Quarterly Journal of Experimental Psychology,* 20 (1), 20–29.

111

Harrison, R. H. 1970. Effect of subliminal shock conditioning on recall. *Journal of Abnormal Psychology,* 75 (1), 19–29.

Hart, L. June 1973. The effect of noxious subliminal stimuli on the modification of attitudes toward alcoholism: A pilot study. *British Journal of Addiction,* 68 (2), 87–90.

Hayden, B., and Silverstein, R. 1983. The effects of tachistoscopic oedipal stimulation on competitive dart throwing. *Psychological Research Bulletin,* Lund Univ., 23 (1), 12.

Heilbrun, K. S. Oct. 1980. The effects of subliminally presented oedipal stimuli on competitive performance. *Dissertation Abstracts International,* 41 (4–B), 1506.

Henley, S. 1975. Cross-model effects of subliminal verbal stimuli. *Scandinavian Journal of Psychology,* 16 (1), 30–36.

Henley, S. H. Nov. 1976. Responses to homophones as a function of cue words on the unattended channel. *British Journal of Psychology,* 67 (4), 559–67.

Henley, S. H., and Dixon, N. F. June 1976. Preconscious processing in schizophrenics: An exploratory investigation. *British Journal Medical Psychology,* 49 (2), 161–6.

Henley, S. H., and Dixon, N. F. Nov. 1974. Laterality differences in the effect of incidental stimuli upon evoked imagery. *British Journal of Psychology,* 65 (4), 529–36.

Henley, S. R. Mar. 1984. Unconscious perception revisited: A comment on Merikle's (1982) paper. *Bulletin of the Psychonomic Society,* 22 (2), 121–24.

Herrick, R. M. Oct. 1973. Increment thresholds for multiple identical flashes in the peripheral retina. *Journal of the Optical Society of America,* 63 (10), 1261–65.

Hines, K. S. May 1978. Subliminal psychodynamic activation of oral dependency conflicts in a group of hospitalized male alcoholics. *Dissertation Abstracts International,* 38 (11–B), 5572.

Hoban, P. July 1984. Subliminal software. *Omni,* 6 (1), 30.

Hobbs, S. Sept. 1984. The effects of subliminal oedipal and symbiotic gratification fantasies on racial attitudes. *Dissertation Abstracts International,* 45 (3–B), 1018.

Hodorowski, L. Feb. 1986. The symbiotic fantasy as a therapeutic agent: An experimental comparison of the effects of four symbiotic contexts on manifest pathology in differentiated schizophrenics. *Dissertation Abstracts International,* 46 (8–B), 2810.

112

Hoffman, J. S. June 1986. Review of the subliminal psychodynamic activation method. Doctor of Psychology research paper, Biola Univ.

Holtzman, D. Nov. 1975. Recall and importations on a word test primed by a subliminal stimulus. *Dissertation Abstracts International,* 36 (5–B), 2473.

Hovsepian, W., and Quatman, G. Feb. 1978. Effects of subliminal stimulation on masculinity-femininity ratings of a male model. *Perceptual and Motor Skills,* 46(1), 155–61.

Hull, E. I. Oct. 1976. Ego states characteristic of enhanced utilization of subliminal registrations. *Dissertation Abstracts International,* 37 (4–B), 1903–04.

Hutchison, M. 1986. *Megabrain.* Ballantine Books.

Hylton, R. L. Sept. 1979. A comparison of the effects of aural arousal on the verbal learning of normal and learning disabled elementary school pupils. *Dissertation Abstracts International,* 40 (3–B), 1393.

Jackson, J. M. Nov. 1983. A comparison of the effects of subliminally presented fantasies of merger with each parent on the pathology of male and female schizophrenics. *Dissertation Abstracts International,* 43 (5–B), 1616–17.

Journal of Advertising Research. Feb. 1979, pp. 55–57. Whether subliminal perception influences behavior is examined by J. Saegert of Univ. of Texas at San Antonio.

Jus, A., and Jus, K. 1967. Neurophysiologic studies of the "unconscious" (thresholds of perception and elements of the "unconscious" in the production of conditioned reflexes). *Zh Nevropatol Psikhiatr (USSR), 67 (12), 1809–15.*

Kaley, H. W. Oct. 1970. The effects of subliminal stimuli and drive on verbal responses and dreams. *Dissertation Abstracts International,* 31 (4–B), 2284.

Kaplan, R.; Thornton, P.; and Silverman, L. Nov. 1985. Further data on the effects of subliminal symbiotic stimulation on schizophrenics. *Journal of Nervous and Mental Disease,* 173 (11), 658–66.

Kaplan, R. B. Sept. 1976. The symbiotic fantasy as a therapeutic agent: An experimental comparison of the effects of three symbiotic elements on manifest pathology in schizophrenics. *Dissertation Abstracts International,* 37 (3–B), 1437–38.

113

Kaser, V.A. July 1986. The effects of an auditory subliminal message upon the production of images and dreams. *Journal of Nervous and Mental Disease,* 174 (7), 397–407.

Katz, Y. Oct. 1965. Subliminal perception and the creative preconscious. *Dissertation Abstracts International,* 34 (4–B), 1751.

Kaye, M. M. Sept. 1975. The therapeutic value of three merging stimuli for male schizophrenics. *Dissertation Abstracts International,* 36 (3–B), 1438–39.

Kennedy, R. S. Apr. 1971. A comparison of performance on visual and auditory monitoring tasks. *Human Factors,* 13 (2), 93–97.

Key, W. 1981. *Clam Plate Orgy.* New York: Signet.

Key, W. 1974. *Subliminal Seduction.* New York: Signet.

Kilbourne, W. E.; Painton, S.; and Ridley, D. 1985. The effect of sexual embedding on responses to magazine advertisements. *Journal of Advertising,* 14 (2), 48–55.

Kleespies, P., and Wiener, M. Aug. 1972. The "orienting reflex" as an input indicator in "subliminal" perception. *Perceptual and Motor Skills,* 35 (1), 103–10.

Klein, G. S. 1970. *Perception, Motives and Personality.* New York: Knopf.

Klein, G. S. 1956. Perception, motives and personality: A clinical perspective. In J. L. McCary, ed., *Psychology of Personality.* New York: Logos.

Klein, G. S.; Spence, D. P.; Holt, R. R.; and Gourevitch, S. 1958. Cognition without awareness: Subliminal influences upon conscious thought. *Journal of Abnormal Social Psychology,* 54.

Klein, S., and Moricz, E. 1969. A study of the effect of threshold stimuli. *Magyar Pszichologiai Szemle,* 26 (2), 198–206.

Kleinbrook, W. L. Feb. 1985. Pastoral considerations regarding the use of subliminal psychodynamic activation. *Dissertation Abstracts International,* 45 (8–A), 2555.

Kolers, P. A. Sept. 1972. Subliminal stimulation in simple and complex cognitive processes. *Dissertation Abstracts International,* 33 (3–B), 1269.

Kostandov, E. A. 1977. Cortical evoked potentials to emotional words (supraliminal and subliminal). *Activities Nervosa Superior,* 19 (4), 301–2.

Kostandov, E. A. 1973. The effect of negative emotions on perception. *Voprosy Psikhologii* (USSR), 19 (6), 60–72.

114

Kostandov, E. A. Mar.-Apr. 1970. Perception and subliminal reactions to unrecognized stimuli. *Zh Vyssh Nerv Deiat* (USSR), 20 (2), 441–9.

Kostandov, E. A. 1969. The effect of emotional excitation on auditory threshold and subliminal reactions. *Zh Vyssh Nerv Deiat* (USSR), 19 (3), 462–70.

Kostandov, E. A. May-June 1968. The effect of unrecognized emotional verbal stimuli. *Zh Vyssh Nerv Deiat* (USSR), 19 (3), 371–80.

Kostandov, E. A., and Arzumanov, IuL. July 1986. The influence of subliminal emotional words on functional hemispheric asymmetry. *International Journal of Psychophysiology,* 4 (2), 143–47.

Kostandov, E. A.; Arzumanov, J.; Vazhnova, T.; Reschikova, T.; Shostakovich, G. Oct.-Dec. 1980. *Pavlov Journal of Biological Science,* 15 (4), 142–50.

Kostandov, E. A., and Arzumanov, IuL. May-June 1978. Conditioned reflex mechanism of unconscious decision making. *Zh Vyssh Nerv Deiat,* 28 (3), 542–8.

Kostandov, E. A., and D'iachkova, G. I. Mar.-Apr. 1971. Evoked potentials of the human cerebral cortex to recognized and unrecognized auditory signals. *Neirofiziologiia* (USSR), 3 (2), 115–22.

Krass, P. Spring 1980–81. Computers that would program people. *Business and Society Review,* 37, 62–64.

Krass, P. Jan. 1981. You will read this article. *Output,* 1 (11), 36–38.

Kreitler, H., and Kreitler, S. Dec. 1974. Optimization of experimental ESP results. *Journal of Parapsychology,* 38, 383–92.

Kreitler, H., and Kreitler, S. Sept. 1973. Subliminal perception and extrasensory perception. *Journal of Parapsychology,* 37 (3), 163–88.

Leclerc, C., and Freibergs, V. Aug. 1971. The influence of perceptual and symbiotic subliminal stimuli on concept formation. *Canadian Journal of Psychology* (Canada), 25 (4), 292–301.

Ledford, B. P. Aug. 1978. The effects of thematic content of rheostatically controlled visual subliminals upon the receiving level of the affective domain of learners.

Ledford, B. R., and Ledford, S. Y. Nov. 1985. The effects of preconscious cues upon the automatic activation of self-esteem of selected middle school students. Requirement for Project 1246. Tucson Unified School District.

115

Lee, I.; Tyrer, P.; Horn, S. Oct. 1983. A comparison on subliminal, supraliminal and faded phobic cinefilms in the treatment of agoraphobia. *British Journal of Psychiatry,* 143, 356–61.

Lee, I., and Tyrer, P. Jan. 1980. Responses of chronic agoraphobics to subliminal and supraliminal phobic motion pictures. *Journal of Nervous and Mental Disease,* 168 (1), 34–40.

Leiter, E. 1982. The effects of subliminal activation of aggressive and merging fantasies in differentiated and nondifferentiated schizophrenics. *Psychological Research Bulletin,* Lund Univ., 22 (7), 21.

Leiter, E. Feb. 1974. A study of the effects of subliminal activation of merging fantasies in differentiated and nondifferentiated schizophrenics. *Dissertation Abstracts International,* 34 (8–B) 4022–23.

Levy, S. Apr. 1984. The selling of subliminal. *Popular Computing,* 8 (6), 70, 75–78.

Libet, B.; Alberts, W. W.; and Wright, E. W. 1976. Responses of human somatosensory cortex to stimuli below threshold for conscious sensation. *Science,* 158 (3808), 1597–1600.

Lieberman, H. J. May 1975. A study of the relationship between developmentally determined personality and associated thought styles and tachistoscopic exposure time as reflected in conflict resolution. *Dissertation Abstracts International,* 35(11–B), 5670–71.

Linehan, E., and O'Toole, J. Mar. 1982. Effect of subliminal stimulation of symbiotic fantasies on college student self-disclosure in group counseling. *Journal of Counseling Psychology,* 29 (2), 151–57.

Litwack, T. R.; Wiedemann, C. F.; and Yager, J. Feb. 1979. The fear of object loss, responsiveness to subliminal stimuli, and schizophrenic psychopathology. *Journal of Nervous and Mental Disease,* 167 (2), 79–90.

Lodl, C. M. Mar. 1981. The effects of subliminal stimuli of aggressive content upon the analytic/field-independent cognitive style. *Dissertation Abstracts International,* 41 (9–B), 3559–60.

Lofflin, J. 20 Mar. 1988. Help from the hidden persuaders. *New York Times.*

Lomangino, L. F. 1969. Depiction of subliminally and supraliminally presented aggressive stimuli and its effects on the cognitive functioning of schizophrenics. *Dissertation Abstracts International,* 30 (4–B), 1900–01.

Lorenzo G. J. Jan.-Feb. 1985. Subliminal stimuli, unconscious psychopathological behavior, diagnostic and therapeutic implications. U Autonoma de Madrid, Facultad de Psicologia, Spain, 6 (1), 30–40.

Lozanov, G. 1978. *Suggestology and Outlines of Suggestopedy.* New York: Gordon and Breach.

McCormack, J. J. Dec. 1980. Effects of gender, intensity, and duration of sex-related visual subliminals upon the submission of controlled attention. *Dissertation Abstracts International,* 41 (6–A), 2409–10.

McGinley, L. 1 Jan. 1986. Uncle Sam believes messages about mom help calm nerves. *Wall Street Journal.*

McGreen, P. J. May 1986. The effects of father absence on affective responses to subliminal symbiotic messages. *Dissertation Abstracts International,* 46 (11–B), 4021–22.

McLaughlin, M. 2 Feb. 1987. Subliminal tapes urge shoppers to heed the warning sounds of silence: 'Don't steal.' *New England Business,* 9 (2), 36–37.

McNulty, J. A.; Deckrill, F. J.; and Levy, B. A. Mar. 1967. The subthreshold perception of stimulus-meaning. *American Journal of Psychology* (U. S.), 90 (1), 28–40.

Magri, M. B. Aug. 1979. Effects of sexual guilt upon affective responses to subliminal sexual stimuli. *Dissertation Abstracts International,* 40 (2–B), 926.

Maltz, M. 1960. *Psychocybernetics.* New York: Simon and Schuster.

Marcel, A. J. Apr. 1983. Conscious and unconscious perception: experiments on visual masking and word recognition. *Cognitive Psychology,* 15 (2), 197–237.

Marketing (Canada's Weekly Newspaper of Marketing Communications). 19 Jan. 1987, pp. 1, 3. CRTC changes mind on television rules.

Marketing Communications. Apr. 1985, p. 8. Subliminal testing: 25 years later.

Marketing News. 15 Mar. 1985, pp. 5–6. Threshold messaging touted as antitheft measure.

Martin, A. Dec. 1975. The effect of subliminal stimulation of symbiotic fantasies on weight loss in obese women receiving behav-

117

ioral treatment. *Dissertation Abstracts International,* 36 (6–B), 30354–55.

Mendelsohn, E. M. Sept. 1981. The effects of stimulating symbiotic fantasies on manifest pathology in schizophrenics: A reverse formulation. *Journal of Nervous and Mental Disease,* 169 (9), 580–90.

Mendelsohn, E. M. June 1980. Responses of schizophrenic men to subliminal psychodynamic stimuli. *Dissertation Abstracts International,* 40 (12–B), 5820–21.

Mendelsohn, E., and Silverman, L. H. 1982. Effects of stimulating psychodynamically relevant unconscious fantasies on schizophrenic psychopathology. *Schizophrenia Bulletin,* 8 (3), 532–47.

Merchandising. Dec. 1983, p. 42. Stimutech (E. Lansing, Michigan) launches Expando-Vision, a device that delivers subliminal messages via computer.

Merikle, P. M. Mar. 1982. Unconscious perception revisited. *Perception and Psychophysics,* 31 (3), 298–301.

Meyers, H. G. Feb. 1982. The effects of a double bind induced by conflicting visual and auditory subliminal stimuli. *Dissertation Abstracts International,* 42 (8–B), 3432.

Mitchell, M. S. June 1985. The effects of subliminally presented praise and reprobation stimuli on willingness to self-disclose. *Dissertation Abstracts International,* 45 (12–B), 3986.

Mofield, J. P. Mar. 1986. Response of blood pressure to relaxation and subliminal suggestion. *Dissertation Abstracts International,* 46 (9–A), 2632.

Molfese, D. Nov. 1985. When is a word a word? *Psychology Today.*

Moore, T. E. July 1985. Subliminal delusion. *Psychology Today,* 19 (2), 10.

Moore, T. E. Spring 1982. Subliminal advertising: What you see is what you get. *Journal of Marketing,* 46 (2), 38–47.

Mopiarty, J. B. 1968. Cognitive functioning of schizophrenics as affected by aggressive stimuli subliminally and supraliminally presented. *Dissertation Abstracts International* , 29 (2–B), 775.

Morgan, P., and Morgan, D. L. 1988. *Subliminal Research: Bibliography and Review.* Center for Independent Research, Clarion Univ.

Moroney, E., and Bross, M. Feb. 1984. Effect of subliminal visual material on an auditory signal detection task. *Perceptual and Motor Skills,* 58 (1), 103–13.

Morrison, A. P. 1982. Reflections on "unconscious oneness fantasies." *International Forum for Psychoanalysis,* 1 (2), 167–80.

Morse, R. C., and Stoller, D. Sept. 1982. The hidden message that breaks habits. *Science Digest,* 90 (1), 28.

Mullins, W. W. Apr. 1978. Convexity theorem for subthreshold stimuli in linear models of visual contrast detection. *Journal of the Optical Society of America,* 68 (4), 456–59.

Murch, G. M. 1967. Aftereffects of subliminal stimulation as a function of the delay between stimulus presentation and reaction to it. *Zeitschrift Für Experimentelle und Angewandte Psychologie,* 1 (3), 463–73.

Murch, G. M. 1967. Temporal gradients of responses to subliminal stimuli. *Psychological Record,* 17 (4), 483–91.

Murch, G. M. 1965. A set of conditions for a consistent recovery of a subliminal stimulus. *Journal of Applied Psychology* (U. S.), 49 (4), 257–60.

Mykel, N. B. Feb. 1977. Emergence of unreported stimuli into imagery as a function of laterality of presentation. *Dissertation Abstracts International,* 37 (8–B), 4156.

Mykel, N., and Daves, W. F. May 1979. Emergence of unreported stimuli into imagery as a function of laterality of presentation: A replication and extension of research by Henley and Dixon (1974). *British Journal of Psychology,* 70 (2), 253–58.

Nelson, J. Messages hidden in music are being widely used to combat shoplifting—and much more. *National Enquirer,* 25.

News release. Oct. 1984, pp. 1–4. Controversial 'brainwashing' and self-hypnosis software release to public.

Nicholson, H. E. Mar. 1980. The effect of contradictory subliminal stimuli and sensitization thereto upon viewers' perception of videotaped testimony. *Dissertation Abstracts International,* 40 (9–A), 4802.

Nissenfeld, S. M. Jan. 1980. The effects of four tapes of subliminal stimuli on female depressives. *Dissertation Abstracts International,* 40 (7–B), 3412–13.

119

Novomeysky, A. Mar. 1984. On the possible effect of an experimenter's subliminal or telepathic influence on dermo-optic sensitivity. *PSI Research,* 3 (1), 8–15.

O'Grady, M. June 1977. Effect of subliminal pictorial stimulation on skin resistance. *Perceptual and Motor Skills,* 44 (3), 1051–56.

Olson, M. C. Mar. 1975. Subliminal messages in advertising. Paper presented at the Annual Meeting of the Conference on English Education (13th, Colorado Springs, Colo., Mar. 20–22, 1975).

Ostrander, S., and Schroeder, L. 1985. *Subliminal Report.* New York: Superlearning.

Ostrander, S., and Schroeder, L. 1980. *Superlearning.* New York: Delta.

Ostrander, S., and Schroeder, L. 1970. *Psychic Discoveries Behind the Iron Curtain.* Englewood Cliffs, N.J.: Prentice-Hall, Inc.

Output. Jan. 1981, pp. 36–38. Experiments in subliminal communication continue.

Overbeeke, C. J. Feb. 1986. Changing the perception of behavioral properties by subliminal presentation. *Perceptual and Motor Skills,* 62 (1), 255–58.

Packard, V. 1957. *Hidden Persuaders.* New York: Affiliated Publishers.

Packard, V. Feb. 1981. The new (and still hidden) persuaders. *Reader's Digest,* 118 (4), 120.

Packer, S. B. July 1984. The effect of subliminally stimulating fantasies aimed at gratifying symbiotic and sanctioning aggressive strivings on assertiveness difficulties in women. *Dissertation Abstracts International,* 459 (1–B), 361.

Pajurkova-Flannery, E. M. Oct. 1979. Subliminal perception in the context of functional hemispheric asymmetries. *Dissertation Abstracts International,* 40 (4–B), 1870.

Palmatier, J. R. Jan. 1981. The effects of subliminal stimulation of symbiotic fantasies on the behavior therapy treatment of smoking. *Dissertation Abstracts International,* 41 (7–B), 2774–75.

Palmatier, J. R., and Bronstein, P. H. Dec. 1980. Effects of subliminal stimulation of symbiotic merging fantasies on behavioral treatment of smokers. *Journal of Mental and Nervous Disorders,* 168 (12), 15–20.

Palumbo, R., and Gillman, I. Dec. 1984. Effects of subliminal activation of Oedipal fantasies on competitive performance: A rep-

120

lication and extension. *Journal of Mental and Nervous Disorders,* 172 (12), 737–41.

Parker, K. A. Jan. 1982. Effects of subliminal symbiotic stimulation on academic performance: Further evidence on the adaptation-enhancing effects of oneness fantasies. *Journal of Counseling Psychology,* 29 (1), 19–28.

Parker, K. A. June 1978. The effects of subliminal merging stimuli on the academic performance of college students. *Dissertation Abstracts International,* 38 (12–B), 6168.

Pfanner, D. A. May 1983. Sensitivity to subliminal stimulation: An investigation of subject variables and conditions affecting psychodynamic and derivative recovery response. *Dissertation Abstracts International,* 43 (11–B), 3739.

Philpott, A., and Wilding, J. Nov. 1979. Semantic interference from subliminal stimuli in a dichoptic viewing situation. *British Journal of Psychology,* 70 (4), 559–63.

Powell, R. C. Apr. 1979. The "subliminal" versus the "subconscious" in the American acceptance of psychoanalysis, 1906–1910. *Journal History Behavioral Science,* 15 (2), 155–65.

Providence *Journal.* 18 Feb. 1986, Sec B, p. 1. Enter a quiet voice against shoplifting.

Pushkash, M. June 1981. Effect of the content of visual presented subliminal stimulation on semantic and figural learning task performance. *Dissertation Abstracts International,* 41 (12–A), 5036.

Rao, P. K., and Rao, K. R. Sept. 1982. Two studies of ESP and subliminal perception. *Journal of Parapsychology,* 46 (3), 285–207.

Rees, W. J. Nov. 1971. On the terms "subliminal perception" and "subception." *British Journal of Psychology,* 62 (4), 501–4.

Richardson, M. V. Dec. 1981. The effects of subliminal implantation in written material on the decision-making process. *Dissertation Abstracts International,* 42 (6–A), 2592.

Robertson, S. R. May 1983. The effect of subliminal merging stimuli on field dependence. *Dissertation Abstracts International,* 43 (11–B), 3741.

Romberg, L. 1975. *Workings of Your Mind.* Burlington, Ontario: Audio Cybernetics.

Roney-Dougal, S. July-Aug. 1981. The interface between psi and subliminal perception. *Parapsychology Review,* 12 (4), 12–18.

Rose, C. 1985. *Accelerated Learning.* Great Britain.

Ross, D. L. Dec. 1978. The effects of subliminal oedipal stimulation on competitive performance in college men. *Dissertation Abstracts International,* 39 (6–B), 3005.

Roufs, J.A., and Pellegrino Van Stuyvenberg, J.A. 1976. Gain curve of the eye to subliminal sinusoidal modulation. *IPO Annual Progress Report,* 11, 56–63.

Rudolph, J. R. Oct. 1970. Selective subliminal perception relative to approach/avoidance tendencies. *Dissertation Abstracts International,* 31 (4–A), 1695.

Ruzumna, J. S. 1969. The effect of cognitive control on responsiveness to subliminal stimulation in social situations. *Dissertation Abstracts International,* 30 (1–B), 373–74.

Sackeim, H. A., and Packer, G. Dec. 1977. Hemisphericity, cognitive set, and susceptibility to subliminal perception. *Journal of Abnormal Psychology,* 86 (6), 624–30.

Saegert, J. Feb. 1979. Another look at subliminal perception. *Journal of Advertising Research,* 19 (1), 55–57.

Schmeidler, G. 1986. Subliminal perception and ESP: Order in diversity? *The Journal of the American Society of Psychical Research,* 80 (3).

Schmidt, J. M. Nov. 1981. The effects of subliminally present anaclitic and introjective stimuli on normal young adults. *Dissertation Abstracts International,* 42 (5–B), 2081.

Schurtman, R.; Palmatier, J. R.; and Martin, E. S. Oct. 1982. On the activation of symbiotic gratification fantasies as an aid in the treatment of alcoholics. *International Journal of Addiction,* 17 (7), 1157–74.

Schwartz, M., and Rem, M. A. July 1975. Does the averaged evoked response encode subliminal perception? *Psychophysiology,* 12 (4), 390–94.

Shevrin, H. July 1975. Does the average evoked response encode subliminal perception? Yes. A reply to Schwartz and Rem. *Psychology* 12 (4), 395–98.

Shevrin, H. 1973. Brain wave correlates of subliminal stimulation, unconscious attention, primary- and secondary-process thinking, and repressiveness. *Psychological Issues,* 8 (2), Mono. 30) 56–87.

Shevrin, H., and Dickman, S. May 1980. The psychological unconscious: A necessary assumption for all psychological theory? *American Psychologist,* 35 (5), 421–34.

Shevrin, H.; Smith, W. H.; Fitzler, D. E. Mar. 1971. Average evoked response and verbal correlates of unconscious mental processes. *Psychophysiology,* 8 (2), 149–62.

Shevrin, H.; Smith, W. H.; and Fritzler, D. E. 1970. Subliminally stimulated brain and verbal responses of twins differing in repressiveness. *Journal of Abnormal Psychology,* 76 (1), 39–46.

Shevrin, H.; Smith, W. H.; and Hoobler, R. 1970. Direct measurement of unconscious mental process: Average evoked response and free association correlates of subliminal stimulation. *Psychological Association,* 5 (Pt. 2), 543–44.

Shevrin, H.; Smith, W. H.; and Fritzler, D. E. 1969. Repressiveness as a factor in the subliminal activation of brain and verbal responses. *Journal of Nervous and Mental Disease,* 149 (3), 2261–69.

Shevrin, H., and Fritzler, D. E. 1968. Visual evoked response correlates of unconscious mental processes. *Science,* 161 (3838), 295–98.

Shevrin, H., and Fisher, C. 1967. Changes in the effects of awaking subliminal stimulus as a function of dreaming and nondreaming sleep. *Journal of Abnormal Psychology,* 72 (4), 362–68.

Shifren, I. W. Apr. 1982. The interaction between hemispheric preference and the perception of subliminal auditory and visual symbiotic gratification stimuli. *Dissertation Abstracts International,* 42 (10–B), 4211,12.

Silverman, L. H. Nov. 1985. Comments on three recent subliminal psychodynamic activation investigations (letter). *Journal of Abnormal Psychology,* 94 (4), 640–48.

Silverman, L. H. 1985. Research on psychoanalytic psychodynamic propositions. Special Issue: Current thinking in psychoanalysis. *Clinical Psychology Review,* 5 (3), 247–57.

Silverman, L. H. 1980. A comprehensive report of studies using the subliminal psychodynamic activation method. *Psychological Research Bulletin,* Lund Univ., 20 (3), 22.

Silverman, L. H. 1980a. Is subliminal psychodynamic activation in trouble? *Journal of Abnormal Psychology.*

Silverman, L. H. 1980b. A comprehensive report of studies using the subliminal psychodynamic activation method. *Psychological Research Bulletin,* 2 (3).

Silverman, L. H. Apr. 1979. The unconscious fantasy as therapeutic agent in psychoanalytic treatment. *Journal of American Academic Psychoanalysis,* 7 (2), 189–218.

Silverman, L. H. 1979. Two unconscious fantasies as mediators of successful psychotherapy. *Psychotherapy: Theory and Practice,* 16, 215–230.

Silverman, L. H. 1978. Further comments on matters relevant to investigations of subliminal phenomena: A reply. *Perceptual and Motor Skills,* 27 (3), 1343–50.

Silverman, L. H. Sept. 1976. Psychoanalytic theory: "The reports of my death are greatly exaggerated." *American Psychologist,* 31 (9), 621–37.

Silverman, L. H. 1975. On the role of laboratory experiments in the development of the clinical theory of psychoanalysis: Data on the subliminal activation of aggressive and merging wishes in schizophrenics. *International Review of Psycho-Analysis,* 2 (1), 43–64.

Silverman, L. H. Dec. 1975. An experimental method for the study of unconscious conflict: A progressive report. *British Journal of Medical Psychology,* 8 (4), 291–98.

Silverman, L. H. 1972. Drive stimulation and psychopathology: On the conditions under which drive-related external events evoke pathological reactions. *Psychoanalysis and Contemporary Science,* 1, 306–26.

Silverman, L. H. Mar. 1971. An experimental technique for the study of unconscious conflict. *British Journal of Medical Psychology,* 44 (1), 17–25.

Silverman, L. H. Jan. 1970. Further experimental studies of dynamic propositions in psychoanalysis: On the function and meaning of regressive thinking. *Journal of the American Psychoanalytic Association,* 18 (1), 102–24.

Silverman, L. H. Apr. 1966. A technique for the study of psychodynamic relationships: the effects of subliminally presented aggressive stimuli on the production of pathological thinking in a schizophrenic population. *Journal of Consulting Psychology* (U. S.), 30 (2), 103.

Silverman, L. H., and Lachmann, F. M. Jan. 1985. The therapeutic properties of unconscious oneness fantasies: Evidence and treatment implications. *Contemporary Psychoanalysis,* 21 (1), 91–115.

Silverman, L. H., and Weinberger, J. Dec. 1985. Mommy and I are one. Implications for psychotherapy. *American Psychology,* 40 (12), 1296–308.

Silverman, L. H.; Lachmann, F. M.; and Milich, R. H. 1984. Unconscious oneness fantasies: Experimental findings and implications for treatment. *International Forum for Psychoanalysis,* 1 (2), 107–52.

Silverman, L. H.; Lachmann, F. M.; and Milich, R. H. 1984. In response. *International Forum for Psychoanalysis,* 1 (2), 205–217.

Silverman, L. H.; Martin, A.; Ungaro, R.; and Mendelsohn, E. June 1978. Effect of subliminal stimulation of symbiotic fantasies on behavior modification treatment of obesity. *Journal of Consulting and Clinical Psychology,* 46 (3), 432–41.

Silverman, L. H.; Ross, D. L.; Adler, J. M.; and Lustig, D. A. June 1978. Simple research paradigm for demonstrating subliminal psychodynamic activation: effects of oedipal stimulation on dart-throwing accuracy in college males. *Journal of Abnormal Psychology,* 87 (3), 341–57.

Silverman, L. H.; Bronstein, A.; and Mendelsohn, E. Spring 1976. The further use of the subliminal psychodynamic activation method for the experimental study of the clinical theory of psychoanalysis: On the specificity of the relationship between symptoms and unconscious. *Psychotherapy: Theory, Research and Practice,* 13 (1), 2–16.

Silverman, L. H.; Levinson, P.; Mendelsohn, E.; Ungaro, R.; and Bronstein, A. A. Dec. 1975. A clinical application of subliminal psychodynamic activation. On the stimulation of symbiotic fantasies as an adjunct in the treatment of hospitalized schizophrenics. *Journal of Nervous and Mental Disease,* 161 (6), 379, 92.

Silverman, L. H.; Frank, S. G.; and Dachinger, P. June 1974. A psychoanalytic reinterpretation of the effectiveness of systematic desensitization: Experimental data bearing on the role of merging fantasies. *Journal of Abnormal Psychology,* 83 (3), 313–18.

Silverman, L. H.; Kwawer, J. S.; Wolitzky, C.; and Coron, M. Aug. 1973. An experimental study of aspects of the psychoanalytic theory of male homosexuality. *Journal of Abnormal Psychology* (U.S.), 82 (1), 178–89.

Silverman, L. H.; Linger, H.; Lustbader, L.; Farrell, J.; and Martin, A. D. June 1972. Effects of subliminal drive stimulation on the speech of stutterers. *Journal of Nervous and Mental Disease* (U. S.), 155 (1), 14–21.

Silverman, L. H.; Candell, P.; Pettit, T. F.; and Blum, F. A. 1971. Further data on effects of aggressive activation and symbiotic merging on ego functioning of schizophrenics. *Perceptual and Motor Skills,* 32, 93–94.

Silverman, L. H., and Candell, P. 1970. On the relationship between aggressive activation, symbiotic merging on ego functioning of schizophrenics. *Perceptual and Motor Skills,* 32, 93–94.

Silverman, L. H., and Candell, P. May 1970. On the relationship between aggressive activation, symbiotic merging, intactness of body boundaries, and manifest pathology in schizophrenics. *Journal of Nervous and Mental Disorders,* 150 (5), 387–99.

Silverman, L. H.; Spiro, R. H.; Weisbert, J. S.; and Candell, P. 1969. The effects of aggressive activation and the need to merge on pathological thinking in schizophrenia. *Journal of Nervous and Mental Disease,* 148 (1), 39–51.

Silverman, L. H., and Silverman, S. E. Feb. 1967. The effects of subliminally presented drive stimuli on the cognitive functioning of schizophrenics. *Journal of Projective Techniques Personal Assessment* (U. S.), 31 (1), 78–85.

Silverman, L. H., and Spiro, R. H. June 1967. Further investigation of the effects of subliminal aggressive stimulation on the ego functioning of schizophrenics. *Journal of Projective Techniques Personal Assessment* (U. S.), 31 (3), 225–33.

Silverman, L. H., and Spiro, R. H. 1967. Some comments and data on the partial cue controversy and other matters relevant to investigations of subliminal phenomena. *Perceptual and Motor Skills,* 25 (1), 325–338.

Silverman, L. H., and Goldweber, A. M. 1966. A further study of the effects of subliminal aggressive stimulation on thinking. *Journal of Nervous and Mental Disease,* 143 (6), 463–72.

Silverman, L. H., and Shiro, R. H. Jan. 1963. The effects of subliminal, supraliminal and vocalized aggression on the ego functioning of schizophrenics. *Journal of Nervous and Mental Disease* (U. S.), 146 (1), 50–61.

126

Singh, Y., and Devi, R. M. Jan.-July 1976. Subliminal guessing: A communication of collegiate students. *Psycho-Lingua,* 6 (1–2), 23–28.

Skean, S. R. May 1978. Videotape presentation of subliminal stimulation based on galvanic skin response monitoring: An investigation in counselor education. *Dissertation Abstracts International,* 38 (11–A), 6547.

Smith, C. D. Dec. 1982. Effects of subliminal stimulation on creative thinking. *Dissertation Abstracts International,* 43 (6–B), 2004.

Smith, G. J.; Gudmund, J.; Carlsson, I.; and Danielsson, A. 1985. Identification with another person: Manipulated by means of subliminal stimulation. *Scandinavian Journal of Psychology,* 26 (1), 74–87.

Smith, G. J., and Danielsson, A. 1979. The influence of anxiety on the urge for aesthetic creation: An experimental study utilizing subliminal stimulation and a percept-genetic technique. *Psychological Research Bulletin,* Lund Univ., 19 (3–4), 36.

Smith, G. J., and Danielsson, A. 1979. A test of identification using subliminal stimulation in a metacontrast design: Preliminary validation with sensitive-paranoid and borderline subjects. *Psychological Research Bulletin,* Lund Univ., 19 (9–10), 23.

Smith, R. B. Apr. 1979. The effects of the incidental perception of rhythm on task performance and mood. *Dissertation Abstracts International,* 39 (10–B), 5049–50.

Soininen, K., and Jarvilehto, T. Nov. 1983. Somatosensory evoked potentials associated with tactile stimulation at detection threshold in man. *Electroencephalogr Clinical Neurophysiology,* 56 (5), 494–500.

Somekh, D. E. Nov. 1976. The effect of embedded words in a brief visual display. *British Journal of Psychology,* 67 (4), 529–35.

Somekh, D. E., and Wilding, J. M. Aug. 1973. Perception without awareness in a dichoptic viewing situation. *British Journal of Psychology,* 64 (3), 339–49.

Sommer, L. Mar. 1986. The effects of subliminal psychodynamic activation on verbal time estimation. *Dissertation Abstracts International,* 46 (9–B), 3231.

Spence, D. P. 1983. Subliminal effects on lexical decision time. *Archiv für Psychologie,* 135 (1), 67–72.

Spence, D. P. 1967. Subliminal perception and perceptual defense: 2 sides of a single problem. *Behavioral Science,* 12 (3), 183–93.

Spence, D. P. and Smith, G. J. Aug. 1977. Experimenter bias against subliminal perception? Comments on a replication. *British Journal of Psychology,* 68 (3), 279–80.

Spiro, T. W. May 1976. The effects of subliminal symbiotic stimulation and strengthening self boundaries of schizophrenic pathology. *Dissertation Abstracts International,* 36 (11–B), 5818–19.

Stambrook, M., and Martin, D. G. 1983. Brain laterality and the subliminal perception of facial expression. *International Journal Neuroscience,* 18 (1–2), 45–58.

Steinberg, R. J. Oct. 1975. The effects of subliminal mother- need tachistoscopic stimulation on the ego pathology of hospitalized male schizophrenics. *Dissertation Abstracts International,* 36 (4–B), 1934.

Strauch, I., et al. 1976. The impact of meaningful auditory signals on sleeping behavior. *Archiv für Psychologie,* 128 (1–2), 75–95.

Strauss, H. 1968. A phenomenological approach to the subconscious. *Nordisk Psykologi,* 20 (4), 203–6.

Stross, L., and Shevrin, H. Jan. 1969. Hypnosis as a method for investigating unconscious thought processes. A review of research. *Journal of the American Psychoanalytic Assoc* (U.S.), 17 (1), 100–135.

Stross, L., and Shervin, H. 1968. Thought organization in hypnosis and the waking state. *Journal of Nervous and Mental Disease,* 147 (3), 272–88.

Sutphen, D. 1982. Battle for Your Mind (Transcript from speech delivered to World Congress of Hypnotists). Malibu, Calif.: Valley of the Sun Publishing.

Swanson, R. J. May 1981. The effects of oedipally related stimuli in the subliminal psychodynamic activation paradigm: A replication and an extension. *Dissertation Abstracts International,* 41 (11–B), 4279.

Taris, L. J. Nov. 1970. Subliminal perception: An experimental study to determine whether a science concept can be taught subliminally to fourth grade pupils. *Dissertation Abstracts International,* 31 (5–A), 2199.

Taylor, E. 1988. *Subliminal Learning: An Eclectic Approach.* Salt Lake City: Just Another Reality Publishing.

Taylor, E. 1987. *Subliminal Technology.* Salt Lake City: PAR, Inc.

Taylor, E. July 1986. Holistic approach to hypnosis. *Attain*. Springfield, Louisiana.

Thuerer, J. R. Apr. 1985 Computer-assisted spelling: A subliminal methodology to increase cognitive performance and academic self-concept. *Dissertation Abstract International,* 45 (10–A), 3074.

Tomlinson, K. Jan. 1983. Just snore that weight off. Los Angeles, 28 (2), 206.

Trank, D. M. 1976. Subliminal Stimulation: Hoax or Reality? Study prepared at Univ. of Iowa.

Trieber, E. J. Aug. 1984. The effects of supraliminal stimulation combined with subliminal symbiotic stimuli on academic performance. *Dissertation Abstracts International,* 45 (2–B), 688–89.

Trimble, R., and Eriksen, C. W. 1966. "Subliminal cues" and the Muller-type illusion. *Perception and Psychophysics,* 1 (11), 401–4.

Tripe, B. Validity in subliminal messages? Professionals tend to disagree. United Press International.

Tyrer, P.; Lewis, P.; and Lee, I. Feb. 1978. Effects of subliminal and supraliminal stress on symptoms of anxiety. *Journal of Nervous and Mental Disease,* 166 (2), 88–95.

Tyrer, P.; Horn, S.; and Lee, I. Feb. 1978. Treatment of agoraphobia by subliminal and supraliminal exposure to phobiccine film. *Lancet,* 1 (8060), 358–60.

Ungaro, R. Apr. 1982. The role of ego strength and alternative subliminal messages in behavioral treatment of obesity. *Dissertation Abstracts International,* 42 (10–B), 4215–16.

Valind, B., and Valind, L. 1968. Effects of subliminal stimulation on homographs. *Psychological Research Bulletin,* 88, 89.

VandenBoogert, C. 1984. A study of potentials unlimited subliminal persuasion/self-hypnosis tapes. Potentials Unlimited, Inc., Grand Rapids, Michigan.

Varga, M. P. Feb. 1974. An experimental study of aspects of the psychoanalytic theory of elation. *Dissertation Abstracts International,* 34 (8–B), 4062–63.

VideoNews. 22 July 1983, pp. 4–5. Environmental video has introduced a subliminal persuasion videocassette that superimposes low-level video messages on cassette tapes.

Walker, A. Dec. 1979. Music and the unconscious. *British Medical Journal,* 2 (6205), 1641–43.

Wall Street Journal. 3 Star, Eastern (Princeton, N.J.) Edition, Sept. 30, 1983, p. 33. Simutech has introduced a device to change behavior by subliminal suggestion.

Watson, G. B. 1970. Motor response latency as an indicator of subliminal affective stimulation. *Journal of General Psychology,* 82 (2), 139–43.

Watson, J. P. Dec. 1975. An experimental method for the study of unconscious conflict. *British Journal of Medical Psychology,* 49 (4), 299–301.

Wechsler, R. Feb. 1987. A new prescription: Mind over malady. *Discover Magazine.*

West, G. N. July 1985. The effects of auditory subliminal psychodynamic activation on state anxiety. *Dissertation Abstracts International,* 46 (1–B), 319.

Westerlundh, B. 1985. Subliminal influence on imagery: Two exploratory experiments. *Psychological Research Bulletin,* Lund Univ., 24 (6–7), 31.

Whalen, B. Mar. 1985. 'Threshold messaging' touted as antitheft measure. *Marketing News,* 19 (6), 5–6.

Whittaker, R. 1975. Subliminal perception: Myth or magic? *Educational Broadcasting,* 8 (6), 17–22.

Wiener, M., and Kleespies, P. Dec. 1968. Some comments and data on partial cue controversy and other matters relevant to investigations of subliminal phenomena: A rejoinder. *Perceptual and Motor Skills* (U. S.), 27 (3), 847–56.

Williams, L. J., and Evans, J. R. Feb. 1980. Evidence for perceptual defense using a lexical decision task. *Perceptual Motor Skills,* 50 (1), 195–98.

Winnett, R. L. Dec. 1981. The comparative effects of literal metaphorical subliminal stimulation on the activation of oedipal fantasies in dart-throwing performance and word recall tasks. *Dissertation Abstracts International,* 42 (6–B), 2557.

Wolman, B. B., ed. 1973. *Handbook of General Psychology.* Englewood Cliffs, N.J.: Prentice-Hall.

Worthington, A. G. June 1966. Generalization phenomena associated with previous pairings of UCS (shock) and subliminal visual stimuli. *Journal of Personal Social Psychology* (U.S.), 3 (6), 634.

Worthington, A. G., and Dixon, N. F. 1968. Subthreshold perception of stimulus meaning. *American Journal of Psychology,* 81 (3), 453–56.

Zanot, E. J.; Pincus, J. D.; and Lamp, E. J. 1983. Public perceptions of subliminal advertising. *Journal of Advertising,* 12 (1), 39–45.

Zanot, E. J., and Maddox, L. M. July 1983. Subliminal advertising and education. Paper presented at the Annual meeting of the Association for Education in Journalism (65th, Athens, Ohio, July 25–28, 1982).

Zenhausern, R.; Pompo, C.; and Ciaiola, M. Apr. 1974. Simple and complex reaction time as a function of subliminal and supraliminal accessory stimulation. *Perceptual and Motor Skills* (U. S.), 38 (2), 417–18.

Zenhausern, R., and Hansen, K. Apr. 1974. Differential effect of subliminal and supraliminal accessory stimulation on task components in problem-solving. *Perceptual and Motor Skills* (U. S.), 39 (2), 375.

Zenhausern, R.; Ciaiola, M.; and Pompo, C. Aug. 1973. Subliminal and supraliminal accessory stimulation and two trapezoid illusions. *Perceptual and Motor Skills,* 37 (19), 251–56.

Zingirian, M.; Molfino, A.; Levialdi, S.; and Trillo, M. 1971. Monocular and binocular responses to liminal and subliminal stimuli. *Ophthalmologica* (Switzerland), 162 (1), 41–50.

Zuckerman, S. G. June 1981. An experimental study of underachievement: The effects of subliminal merging and success-related stimuli on the academic performance of bright underachieving high school students. *Dissertation Abstracts International,* 41 (12–B), 4699–4700.

Zwosta, M. F., and Zenhausern, R. June 1969. Application of signal detection theory to subliminal and supraliminal accessory stimulation. *Perceptual and Motor Skills* (U. S.), 28 (3), 699–70.